The Military-Industrial Complex

The Military-Industrial Complex

Sidney Lens

PILGRIM PRESS & *THE NATIONAL CATHOLIC REPORTER*

The Military-Industrial Complex is a copublishing
project of Pilgrim Press, the trade imprint of United
Church Press, Philadelphia, Pennsylvania, and *The
National Catholic Reporter*, Kansas City, Missouri.

Much of the enclosed material appeared in a modified
form as a series in *The National Catholic Reporter*.

Contents

The Military-Industrial Complex

CHAPTER ONE

Unmasking the Goliath

The one useful result of the Vietnam War may be that it has finally made the military establishment fair game for criticism. Until the war proved "unwinnable," the Pentagon wore a halo. Its words on weapons, strategy, and budgets were sacrosanct. When it came to the higher mathematics of procurement, its judgment was accepted like a message from Mount Sinai, and the nation followed it from one weapons system to another, from one enlarged budget to another, with humble awe. From 1946 to 1967, according to the statistics of Senator J. William Fulbright, the federal government spent $904 billion, or 57.29 percent of its budget "for military power," and only $96 billion, or 6.08 percent for "social functions," such as education, health, labor and welfare programs, housing and community development.[1] Convincing the American people that they ought to spend nine times as much on guns as on human welfare was an act of mesmerism by the military establishment without parallel. Both the people and Congress rubber-stamped an arsenal of horror that began with the 20-kiloton Hiroshima atom bomb, equivalent to 20,000 tons of dynamite, and escalated to a stockpile of multimegaton hydrogen bombs, equivalent to millions of tons each; that began with a modest bomber plane of limited range and escalated to intercontinental bombers, then unmanned missiles, and finally multi-weapon missiles independently targeted; that began with a capacity to kill a few million people and grew in a single generation, with hydrogen bombs, missiles, and chemical and biological weapons, to a capacity to kill all living things on this planet dozens of times over.

Except for a handful of pacifists, radicals, and, periodically, a few members of Congress, no one questioned the utility or sanity of all this. The Department of Defense alone, not to mention the Atomic Energy Commission (AEC), the National Aeronautics and Space Administration (NASA), and tens of thousands of defense contractors, employed 66,000 scientists and engineers as of 1966.[2] In 1961, when the defense budget was only $44 billion, America was spending $247 for every man, woman, and child in the country on the military, as against $19 per head on foreign economic assistance.[3] Since then the former figure has grown by about two thirds; the latter has declined. As a barometer of the nation's sense of values, the aircraft and missile industry spent $5.4 billion for research and development in 1966, most of it supplied by the federal government, while the Department of Health, Education, and Welfare was allotted a fourth as much.[4] Andrew Hamilton estimates that the Pentagon will spend $30 billion in the next 10 years on three weapons — the F-14A supersonic plane, the Safeguard anti-ballistic missile (ABM), and the Advanced Manned Strategic Aircraft (AMSA). This $3 billion a year, if invested in federal domestic programs, would:

- nearly double federal support for primary and secondary education; or
- double federal job and training programs for the unemployed and disadvantaged; or
- triple the present level of food assistance programs to combat hunger; or
- provide nearly 20 times the present level of federal assistance for urban mass transportation.[5]

"There is something intrinsically obscene," writes former ambassador to India, John Kenneth Galbraith, "in the combination of ill-fed people and well-fed armies deploying the most modern equipment."[6] But the populace, until now at least, has been willing to upgrade war and downgrade hunger, because it was convinced the Pentagon "knew what it was doing."

Vietnam, however, has tarnished the image of infallibility. Defense secretaries and generals kept promising that a few more dollars and a few more men would bring victory, but there has been no victory. In 1953, when the United States was underwriting most of France's expenses against the Viet Minh, Secretary Charles E. Wilson assured all and sundry that "French victory is both possible and probable." Admiral Arthur W. Radford echoed these sentiments: "The French are going to win." Six years later when the French had already lost and new guerrilla movements were rising in South Vietnam, Lieutenant General S. T. Williams gave it as his expert assessment that "the guerrilla threat in Vietnam has receded to a point where one single territorial regiment could handle it." By 1962, when the United States had 8,000 "advisors" in Vietnam and the Ngo Dinh Diem regime was deploying many divisions against the guerrillas, Secretary Robert S. McNamara was "tremendously encouraged" by developments on the fighting front and pledged that there was "no plan for introducing combat forces into South Vietnam." McNamara's subsequent prophecies are notable for their misjudgment: "The corner has been definitely turned toward victory" (May 1963); "The major part of the U.S. military task can be completed by the end of 1965" (October 1963); "We have every reason to believe that plans will be successful in 1964" (December 1963); "The U.S. hopes to withdraw most of its troops from South Vietnam before the end of 1965" (February 1964). And in November 1965, after all these trumpets of near-victory, he announced that "we have stopped losing the war."[7] The same synthetic optimism has come from the lips of Generals Wheeler, Taylor, Westmoreland, and others, to the point where all of it finally lost its credibility. The war was not being won; at best it was stalemated. "The frustration of the United States in Vietnam," commented historian Arnold J. Toynbee, was "one of the wonders of the world."[8]

In the face of this unimpressive record the latent critics of the military rose to the offensive. Wisconsin's Senator William Proxmire and his Subcommittee on Economy in Government began revealing late in 1968, in scathing detail, the Pentagon's proclivity to "excessive costs, burgeoning military budgets, and scandalous performances."[9] With the aid of a few people in the Pentagon itself, such as A. E. Fitzgerald, who were ready to talk regardless of personal consequences, Proxmire's subcommittee has uncovered a miasma of waste, inefficiency, and probably corruption, which draws stern attention to the military's clay feet. Half the Senate, including many hawks of yesteryear — Stuart Symington (Dem.-Mo.) for instance — have joined in opposition to the Safeguard ABM and came within a single vote of defeating it. And journalists by the carload are now working up exposés on the "military-industrial complex" which a year or two ago would have received the silent treatment. The term itself — militaryindustrial complex — has become, for many people, one of opprobrium, and the military has been put to considerable trouble trying to prove there was nothing sinister or conspiratorial about it.

What is still lacking, unfortunately, is a sense of historical perspective. How did the military-industrial complex arise in the first place? What is its role and purpose? Why do we have one now when we didn't have one before? What has it done to our institutions that the old "merchants of death" did not do? How does it affect our future as a nation and as individuals?

These questions are not yet being probed, except by the offstage peace movement. Yet the story of overruns and misused resources may be a beginning to the search for more fundamental answers. It is a story so incredible it leaves conscientious citizens all but wilted.

The Pentagon, it has become evident, wastes the taxpayer's money like the proverbial sailor on a drunken binge. C. H. Danhoff of the Brookings Institution records in his study "Government Contracting and Technological Change" that "during the 1950s virtually all large military contracts . . . ultimately involved costs in excess of original contractual estimates of from 300 to 700 percent."[10]

By all accounts the situation has not improved since then. C. Merton Tyrrell, a former Air Force consultant, told Proxmire's subcommittee in June 196? that the Minuteman II, which was expected to cost $3.3 billion will actually cost $7 billion, an overrun of almost $4 billion. The C-5A cargo plane, built by Lockheed, was bid at $3 billion but will run at least $2 billion more. Eight hundred Mark IIs were first figured at $610 million but are now expected to cost at least $2.5 billion. The SRAM missiles, estimated at $301 million in January 1968, by December 1968 were expected to cost upward of $636 million. The Navy DRSV — deep submersible rescue vessel — which was supposed to be built for $36.5 million for 12 vessels is now priced at $480 million for six; and according to Senator Proxmire there is only a single instance in the last 40 years where such a rescue vessel could have been of use.[11] Defense Secretary Melvin Laird conceded on June 20, 1969 that the overrun on nine projects alone was $3.5 billion — twice as much as the nation spends each year on its antipoverty program. Since 1946 the figure undoubtedly runs into many tens of billions, though no one has yet been permitted to dig into the files of Pentagonia to discover exactly how many.

Ironically, the 22,000 prime contractors who do business with the Department of Defense (DOD) are all fervid advocates of the free enterprise system and competition — except for themselves. Ninety percent of all weapons procurement is now done without competitive bidding — simply by negotiations between a colonel or general and the specific company. The contractor, therefore, makes a low estimate to begin with, so as not to unduly alarm the Secretary of Defense or congressional skeptics, and then goes on to spend two or three times as much, with little fear that the Pentagon will, or can, cancel his order.

The Pentagon, Proxmire shows, treats its industrial allies with regal generosity. It has made available to defense contractors $13.3 billion of government-owned land, buildings, machinery, and materials, saving them the job of financing their own investments. Lockheed, for instance, is building the C-5A cargo plane on government facilities that had an original acquisition cost of $113.8 million. This is a form of "private socialism," in which the public takes the risk, the companies the profit.

The same generosity is evident in patent policy. The federal government pays for the research and development, but it "permits contractors to obtain exclusive patent rights, free of charge, on inventions produced in the performance of government contracts." The Boeing 707 commercial plane was essentially an "offshoot" of the KC-135 military jet tanker. Hundreds of spin-off products, first developed with DOD, NASA, or AEC money, are now being marketed commercially by the corporations, for their own profit.[12] Additionally, DOD sometimes winks an eye at the practice of using government money for nondefense research. A glaring example brought to light involved three firms who were paid $22.4 million for work on the Minuteman, but diverted $18 million of these sums for research that was not remotely connected with either missile or any other defense work. The Pentagon spares no effort — or money — to make its industrial suppliers happy. While they are still fabricating the weapons, contractors may receive substantial "progress" payments, which in effect are interest-free loans. On incurred costs of $1.278 billion, as of December 27, 1968, Lockheed, for instance, was given "progress" payments of $1.207 billion. All it had to raise was $71 million of its own cash for a transaction involving cost and facilities close to a billion and a half dollars. Any nondefense manufacturer in America would give his left eyetooth for terms so favorable.

Yet despite the Government's unbounded benevolence, weapons come off the assembly line "two years later than promised," on the average, and fall far below specifications in the contract. Proxmire reports that "of 13 major aircraft and missile programs with sophisticated electronic systems built for the Air Force and Navy since 1955 at a cost of $40 billion, only four, costing $5 billion, could be relied on to reach a performance level of 75 percent or above of their specifications." Four others, costing $13 billion, "broke down at a performance level which was 75 percent or less than their specifications." Two, for which the taxpayer paid $10 billion, were so poor they had to be scrapped after three years because of "low reliability," and two, costing $2 billion, had to be canceled.[13]

To round out the gaudy picture, at least 68 weapons systems, worth $9 billion, had to be abandoned as unworkable, including the nuclear-powered plane on which $512 million was lost, the B-70 superbomber (a loss of $1.5 billion), the Snark robot bomber ($678 million), the Navaho missile ($680 million), and others.[14] This waste does not include incidents of outright theft such as the disappearance of three million gallons of gasoline in Thailand or innumerable peculations of the same sort in Vietnam.[15]

Editors of the authoritative *Congressional Quarterly*, after interviewing "highly placed sources in the Pentagon," concluded that $10.8 billion could have been cut from the 1969 defense budget without impairing the military posture one iota. A former Pentagon official, Robert S. Benson, puts the figure at $9 billion that could be saved "without reducing our national security or touching those funds earmarked for the war in Vietnam." Proxmire claims further that of the $45.8 billion in "our military supply pipeline," 28 percent, or $12.7 billion, is unneeded excess.

But if waste is monumental it doesn't prevent the inefficient corporations from being lavishly rewarded. A *Washington Post* article of June 17, 1969, reports that "a defense contractor who produced substandard guidance 'brains' for the Minuteman II missile has received an estimated $400 million in additional orders for the same device." Far from being penalized, the contractor was rewarded. As far as profits are concerned, not enough is known about them to be definitive, first because DOD does not make adequate studies on the subject, and second because corporations include civilian and defense work profits in one lump. There are strong indications, however, that the military industrialist does considerably better than his counterpart in the consumer industries. Prof. Murray Weidenbaum made a comparison of large defense firms doing three fourths of their business with the Government and industrial firms of comparable size selling their wares on the commercial market. He found that the former earned 17.5 percent on investment from 1962 to 1965, as against 10.6 percent for the latter.

Admiral Hyman Rickover told the Proxmire subcommittee that propulsion turbine suppliers today insist on profits of 25 percent of costs, where a few years ago they were willing to accept 10 percent. Shipbuilders, he said, have doubled their rate of return in the past two years. According to Colonel A. W. Buesking, "profits based on return on investment in the Minuteman program, from 1958 to 1966, were 43 percent." North American Aviation evidently hit the jackpot, in the opinion of a 1962 tax court, by earning 612 percent and 802 percent profit on its investment in two successive years.

Such tales of greed, waste, and inefficiency would stagger any normal business and any other government agency, but when it comes to "defense" spending the nation has become so accustomed to deferring to the military that tens of billions of dollars seem inconsequential. A proposal by Senator George McGovern and 14 others for an excess profits tax on war production is not likely to garner any support in the defense industry, or in Congress itself for that matter.

There is a hint in the Proxmire hearings that more than human error is involved. In fiscal 1968, says the senator, the 100 companies that did more than two thirds of the prime military work, held on their payrolls "2,072 retired military officers of the rank of colonel or Navy captain or above."[16] Lockheed Aircraft (of C-5A fame) led the pack with 210; Boeing came next with 169; McDonnell Douglas Corporation, 141; General Dynamics, 113; North American Rockwell, 104; General Electric, 89. Retired military officers must be a valuable asset, for in 1959 the 100 largest defense contractors employed only a third as many as today — 721 as against 2,072. Many of the same men who negotiated the lush deals with private business when they wore Pentagon hats used their influence and inside knowledge on behalf of defense companies after retirement. Pentagon regulations forbid a retired officer to "represent anyone other than the United States in connection with a matter in which the United States is a party or has an interest and in which he participated personally and substantially for the Government." But as a Pentagon spokesman points out, no one, to his knowledge, has ever been prosecuted for such conflicts of interest. Admiral William Fechteler, a former chief of naval operations, told a House subcommittee some years ago how he got around this difficulty. As a $30,000 a year employee for General Electric, plus $8,500 incentive pay, plus $12,000 retirement pay from the Navy, he would simply introduce company officials to the Secretary of the Navy or key admirals, and politely leave the room while they talked contracts.[17] If this is not corruption it certainly skirts the thin edges.

What can one say, for instance, of the fact that an Assistant Secretary of Defense, Thomas Morris, went directly from his post as chief procurement officer at the Pentagon to a top job with Litton Industries? In his last full year in government, Morris and his subordinates approved a 250 percent jump in Litton's defense orders, from $180 million to $466 million. Now as a Litton executive he will be dealing with former underlings to raise the ante. With Morris "coaching the Litton team," asks Senator Proxmire, "how objective will Morris' former subordinates be in deciding whether or not to give the big profitable jobs to Litton? . . . Morris' vice-presidency of Litton can be viewed both as a payoff for the huge Pentagon business shifted to Litton in 1968 and as assurance of immense future influence for Litton."[18]

Litton has 49 retired high-ranking officers on its payroll. Retired General Carl A. Spaatz is on its board of directors. John H. Rubel, a senior vice-president, is a former Assistant Secretary of Defense. With all these men opening doors into the right Pentagon office it is little wonder that Litton jumped from thirty-sixth largest prime defense contractor in 1967 to fourteenth in 1968. On the same basis, to a greater or lesser degree, the 2,072 former active officers try to achieve similar results for their companies and are being similarly rewarded.

These are all alarming facts, strongly hinting that aggrandizement has been more important than patriotism in stoking the fires of preparedness. Whether it is or isn't, however, one may be sure that, despite the efforts of Senator Proxmire and others, the full story of waste and corruption in the Pentagon's expenditure of more than a trillion dollars since World War II has not yet been told.

More will undoubtedly come to light in the near future, for Proxmire is an honest man with a passion for fiscal rectitude. Interestingly, he is no antiwar maverick in the tradition of one of his Wisconsin predecessors, Robert M. La Follette. After the 1964 election "Prox" defended Lyndon Johnson against the charge of implementing the Goldwater policy on Vietnam like a parish priest defending his pope. His anti-communism has sometimes been more fierce than that of the Establishment — for instance, in his opposition to aid for independent Yugoslavia on the ground that it is Communist. He believes in most of the clichés of the Cold War, including the need for "preparedness." He is angry at the military-industrial complex only because it is shortchanging the American people; it isn't giving enough "bang for a buck," as one of his speeches puts it.

Important as is the criticism of overruns and similar issues by men like Proxmire, its value is limited and it is not likely to bring any but superficial changes. For if the American people accept the fundamentalist thesis that the military is our bastion of "defense," a few wasted tens of billions will not alarm them into anti-military heresy. DOD will accept some of Proxmire's accounting proposals, such as "zero-cost" budgeting; expenditures will be trimmed a few billion; contractors will be instructed to make more realistic bids — and there the matter will rest.

There are issues far more urgent than cost overruns, however. The military, Senator Fulbright asserts, "is a direct threat to American democracy." Is that true, or is it an exaggeration? Does the military-industrial complex make the United States stronger, as most people claim, or weaker? Does it assure victory — whatever that means — or hasten defeat? For a quarter of a century Americans have accepted without question certain assumptions — about communism and freedom, about Brezhnev, Mao, and Castro, about the ideals of their leaders and generals, about military theories like "deterrence." It is time to ask now, "Are they valid?" In the light of the Pentagon's obvious inadequacy in Vietnam, has it also been wrong in its basic strategy?

"The American people," said Senators Symington, Stephen Young (Dem.-Ohio), and Daniel K. Inouye (Dem.-Hawaii) in a dissent to the ABM, "have lived with fears of a Soviet attack . . . ever since World War II and have expended a thousand billion dollars on defense in recognition of this possible danger. These gigantic expenditures have been detrimental to many other plans, programs, and policies which now also appear vitally important to the security and well-being of this nation."

Journalist I. F. Stone speaks of the same issue much more sharply:

The truth is that we have spent a trillion dollars . . . on a gigantic hoax. The U.S. emerged from World War II, as from World War I, virtually unscathed, enormously enriched and — with the atom bomb — immeasurably more powerful than any nation on earth had ever been. The notion that it was in danger of attack from a devastated Soviet Union with 25 million war dead, a generation behind it in industrial development, was a wicked fantasy. But this myth has been the mainstay of the military and the war machine.[19]

In the September 1969 issue of *Esquire*, Ernest J. Sternglass, professor of radiation physics at the University of Pittsburgh, asserts that if the United States were able to intercept with anti-ballistic missiles the five hundred 25-megaton SS-9 missiles that Secretary Laird claims the Russians soon may have, it would be disastrous. The vast amounts of "long-lived strontium 90 necessarily released into the world's rapidly circulating atmosphere" would kill off all Russian and American infants in the next generation, "thus ending the existence of the Russian people, together with that of all mankind." Sternglass, DOD will no doubt argue, is wrong. But who knows? And what if he is right?

What is needed clearly is a probe of fundamentals. The highest peacetime military budgets of the past ranged from $600 to $900 million a year under Franklin Roosevelt — a rate of expenditure which prompted the liberal *New Republic* to castigate Roosevelt as a "warmonger." Today's level is $80 billion, excluding space expenditures which are defense-related and some cloak-and-dagger funds for the Central Intelligence Agency and similar groups. Forty-four billion of these sums go to 22,000 prime contractors and 100,000 subcontractors for procurement, creating in their wake a vast constituency interested in prolonging the arms race.

The Pentagon puts its wealth at $202.5 billion — a figure which Richard F. Kaufman severely questions because it has "greatly underestimated" the value of land and other items listed at *acquisition* costs a long time ago rather than real worth today.[20] The Pentagon owns 29 million acres of land — almost the size of New York state — plus another 9.7 million acres under the control of the Army Civil Works division, valued, all-told, at $47.7 billion. It is custodian of $100 billion worth of weaponry and $55.6 billion in supplies and plant equipment. Its true wealth undoubtedly ranges from $300 to $400 billion, or about six to eight times the annual after-tax profits of *all* American corporations.

The question is how an institution of these dimensions expanded so mightily in 25 years. It is not enough to say that it "grew like Topsy" or that it is the result of a "conspiracy," because history shows it blossomed with the support and encouragement of the civilian leaders in Washington. It is inconceivable, moreover, that men as conversant with the mechanism of power as our politicians would have yielded such power to the military goliath if they hadn't felt it carried out their own goals. Nor would they have turned their backs on a century and a half of anti-militarist tradition unless they felt they were thereby serving a drastically redefined — and correct — national purpose.

Ever since George Washington, America has been an anti-militarist state. It has engaged in many wars, to be sure — as of 1924 six major ones and 104 minor ones — but it has always been opposed to large standing armies and large military establishments. At the end of the War of the Revolution, Washington dissolved the army entirely and sent it home, leaving defense to the ragged and inept state militia. When he later asked for a small regular force — denied, incidentally — he conceded that a large military "hath ever been considered dangerous to the liberties of a country." In June 1784 Congress passed a resolution in the same vein — that "standing armies in time of peace are inconsistent with the principles of republican governments, dangerous to the liberties of a free people, and generally converted into destructive engines for establishing despotism."

As of 1845, just before the Mexican War, the military contingent stood at 9,000 officers and men; as late as 1904 at a relatively small 53,000; and on the eve of World War II, 139,000. Today there are more than three and a half million in 470 major bases, camps, and installations, and 5,000 lesser ones around the nation, as well as 429 major bases and 2,972 minor ones overseas.[21] The military establishment, far from being dismantled as in previous postwar periods, is increasing its wealth and power from year to year. Even the conclusion of the Korean War in the early 1950s led to a reduction in military spending of only a few billion for two or three years, and since then it has almost doubled. It is now seven times what it was in 1948 and 80 times what it was before World War II.

For good or ill — and in this writer's view, for ill — all this represents a qualitative change in the American way of life. It has concentrated too much unchecked power in too few hands. It has corrupted the process of "government by consent of the governed." It has *necessarily* put us in the same bed with dozens of dictators and established us as a policeman rather than a negotiator in our relations with the rest of the world.

One may say that regrettable as these results may have been they were necessary to curb an aggressor, to defend America from Communist Russia or Communist China — in a nuclear age. But the Soviets did not have an atom bomb until the Cold War was already a few years old, and were not expected to have one, in the view of Lieutenant General Leslie R. Groves, in charge of the American atomic project, for at least five years under the best circumstances, and probably 20 years.[22] Pointing to a potential aggressor begs the question anyway, for we have always had foreign enemies we claimed threatened our security — England, France, England again (in 1812), Spain, Mexico, Germany, Italy, Japan. Moreover in the early days of the Republic both England and France were far more potent than the United States — even with an ocean in the way. Yet we never before tolerated a permanent military establishment of any consequence, and certainly not of the present size. We never before consented, as Eugene McCarthy puts it, to permitting a "Republic within the Republic."

There must be an explanation for the rise of the military-industrial complex, therefore, that goes beyond the issue of security. Or, to say it in another way, the word security must have a connotation somewhat different from what it has had in the past.

CHAPTER TWO

Origins and Purpose

In the orthodox scenario, the military-industrial complex originated with World War II and the sophisticated weaponry needed to win it. The War Department and the War Production Board had to lean on industry to produce planes, cannons, tanks. As electronics and the atom became instruments of war, the university was co-opted to supply brain power. It was a necessary partnership to win a war and save democracy. "If we didn't have a military-industrial complex," says Admiral J. M. Lyle (retired), president of the National Security Industrial Association, "we would have to invent one, for the design and production and maintenance of today's complicated weapons necessarily entails the closest cooperation and communications between the military that requires them and the industry which provides them."[1]

The cooperation between the military, industry, university, labor hierarchy, and other allies, was even more necessary in the postwar period, for in the meantime we had acquired a new enemy — communism — which like the old enemy, but much more vigorously, was bent on world conquest. Regrettably it was essential to maintain and enlarge the military establishment, because as General Mark Clark (retired) put it: "You can't do business with the Commies except by force, and with no appeasement whatsoever."[2] In this pristine tableau the enemy was all bad, we were all good; he stood for dictatorship, we stood for freedom; he aimed at expansion, we at peace. "The Soviet Union," said Presidential candidate Richard M. Nixon on October 17, 1968, "is a power still attempting to expand around the world. The United States, on the other hand, is a power whose goal is only peace. We are not attempting to dominate any part of the world; we are merely trying to assure the right of freedom of choice for other nations."

In this eviscerated image the United States seems to have no ambitions that normal nations have, namely the expansion of power and influence; and its military establishment seems to have no other purpose but to "resist aggression." We are expected to believe that a society based on private profit sternly subordinates this motive in dealing with foreign countries, and that for the first time in history military bases abroad are no longer an instrument of empire-building but of helping harassed peoples achieve "self-determination."

If this is true it is a remarkable transformation of a nation whose history is punctuated by an expansionist elan. George Washington referred to the United States as a "rising empire,"[3] and most of the founding fathers demanded that Canada and the Floridas be incorporated into the United States. "So long as Great Britain shall have Canada, Nova Scotia, and the Floridas, or any of them," John Adams wrote in 1778, "so long will Great Britain be the enemy of the United States. . ."[4] The War of 1812 was in large measure an effort to achieve this goal. America's eyes were cast west, south, and north throughout the nineteenth century, not only in scores of wars to seize Indian territory, but to seize land belonging to Spain, France, England, and Mexico. "We were guided," said Congressman Robert C. Winthrop of Massachusetts — and repeated by President James K. Polk — by "the right of our manifest destiny to spread over this whole continent."[5] A half century later Theodore Roosevelt denied that the United States "feels any land hunger," but insisted that it had, "however reluctantly" the right to "the exercise of an international police power."[6] We had a right to defend uncivilized states, such as Hawaii or Colombia, "from themselves." Under the principles of "dollar diplomacy" which held sway in the ensuing decades the American colossus no longer sought sovereignty over foreign lands but was content to dominate Latin America through economic and political controls, using intervention only as a final expedient.

To think of the United States, then, as a nation which has suddenly foresworn expansion of its influence overseas clashes harshly with the lessons of history and the theorems of many American military and political leaders. "Commerce follows the flag," said Senator Henry Cabot Lodge way back in 1895. And Captain (later Admiral) Alfred T. Mahan, in his oft-quoted work, *The Influence of Sea Power upon History*, advocated a large permanent navy to control the seas and expand American trade. With such a navy, said Mahan, the United States would acquire bases around the world, and colonies as a source of raw materials and commerce.[7]

A more realistic estimate than the orthodox one concerning the role of the military-industrial complex in the postwar period was made by Hanson W. Baldwin, the well-known military correspondent of *The New York Times*, in a December 1947 article for *Harper's* entitled "The Military Moves In":

> Some wise man once wrote that each victorious war costs us a few more of our liberties. Not only does the Government, like an octopus, draw to itself during war extensive new powers, many of which are not repealed when peace comes, but the great emotional upsurge of victory inevitably has the double effect of carrying to new positions of authority the military architects of victory, and encouraging in the rest of us dreams of an expanded "manifest destiny" for our country.

This pithy statement, though incomplete, carries a solid insight into the origins and purpose of the military-industrial complex. The complex, a conglomerate of elites in the War Department, industry, and elsewhere, had begun to accumulate *power* during a victorious war. That power would be put to full use in the subsequent cold war to encourage and implement a mandate of "manifest destiny."

The military, supported by major industrialists, tried as early as World War II to take full charge of the American economy. Donald Nelson, head of the War Production Board, records in his *Arsenal of Democracy* that "from 1942 onward the Army people, in order to get control of our national economy, did their best to make an errand boy of the WPB." A Bureau of the Budget document published in 1946, *The United States at War*, says that the Army tried to gain "total control of the nation, its manpower, its facilities, its economy," and when Roosevelt or Nelson blocked this scheme temporarily, "the military leaders took another approach to secure the same result. . ."[8] Since war expenditures accounted for more than one out of every three dollars of gross national product in 1945 the War Department felt it had a legitimate right to run the economy.

This view was reinforced by business leaders in and out of government — e.g. James Forrestal of Dillon, Read, and Charles E. Wilson of General Electric. What the nation needed, said Wilson in January 1944, was "a permanent war economy." He proposed that every large company choose a liaison man with the armed forces (to be commissioned as a colonel in the reserve), because military preparedness "must be, once and for all, a continuing program and not the creature of an emergency." Under his scheme Congress would be "limited to voting the needed funds" while the military and big business would run the show.

Why did we need a "permanent" war economy? For the record, the American people were told in lurid redundancy that both we and our allies were in danger of a military attack from Soviet Russia. "The Pentagon line," said Colonel William H. Neblett, national president of the Reserve Officers Association, "was that we were living in a state of undeclared emergency; that war with Russia was just around the corner. . ."[9]

Long before the Soviets had acquired their first atom bomb or even tested one, Lieutenant General Leslie R. Groves warned that in the first five hours of an atomic attack 40 million Americans would be killed, and General Carl A. Spaatz explained that it would be too late for defense after the atomic bombs started falling. By drawing this ominous picture the military was able to win approval of a $12 billion budget for fiscal 1948.

But a whole host of scholars — D. F. Fleming, William Appleman Williams, Gabriel Kolko, David Horowitz, Richard Barnet,

Marcus Raskin, to name a few — now question the assumption that the Soviet Union was preparing for a military invasion either of Western Europe or the United States. The Russian dictator, Joseph Stalin, was brutal in dealing with his own people, but it is often forgotten that for a few years after the war, he assumed an exceedingly moderate posture elsewhere. His nation had lost 25 million people in the war, was desperately in need of aid for rebuilding, and continued for a long time to nurture hopes of coexistence. Far from being revolutionary, Stalin in those years put the damper on revolution wherever he could.

The Soviet leader, reports historian Fleming, "scoffed at communism in Germany, urged the Italian Reds to make peace with the monarchy, did his best to induce Mao Tse-tung to come to terms with the Kuomintang and angrily demanded of Tito that he back the monarchy, thus fulfilling his (Stalin's) bargain with Churchill."[10]

While De Gaulle was still in Algeria the communist-led resistance fighters took over the French factories. With their stockpile of weapons and large following they might have attempted a revolutionary seizure of power. But De Gaulle took a plane to Moscow, talked with Stalin, and French Communists thereupon evacuated the factories and submitted to disarming of the partisans. Leftist Communists such as Marty and Thillon never forgave Stalin this "treachery." Another word from Moscow and the danger of revolution abated in Italy, with Italian Communists too relinquishing the factories and submitting to being disarmed.

Communists in this period joined "bourgeois governments" throughout Europe and worked hard to rebuild tattered economies. "The key" to reconstruction in France, wrote Joseph Alsop in July 1946, was "the enthusiastic collaboration of the French Communist Party. The Communists control the most important unions of the C.G.T., the great French confederation of labor unions. Communist leadership has been responsible for such surprising steps as acceptance by the key French unions of a kind of modified piecework system. . . . Reconstruction comes first, is the Party line."[11] The Communists dissuaded their followers in North Africa from taking the path of revolution, thus leaving the field to non-Communist nationalists like Ahmed Ben Bella. Stalin ordered Soviet troops out of Azerbaijan — northwest Iran — thereby liquidating the Communist regime under Jafar Pishevari. He failed to lift a finger while British forces put down an EAM revolt in Greece, a circumstance for which he won lavish praise from no less a personage than Winston Churchill. Stalin, wrote Churchill, "adhered strictly and faithfully to our agreement of October, and during all the long weeks of fighting the Communists in the streets of Athens not one word of reproach came from *Pravda* or *Izvestia*."[12] As for China — according to the British Royal Institute of International Affairs — Stalin tried to dissuade Mao, as late as 1948, from an "all-out offensive to crush the Kuomintang and seize power."[13]

Stalin *did* torpedo democratic elections in Poland and *did* help satellite parties, with small popular followings, to gain the helm in Eastern Europe. In the passions of cold war, however, the American memory is letter perfect on the "broken pledges" of Moscow, but tends toward amnesia on the broken pledges of the West. We forget that in addition to Yalta, one of the fundamental documents of World War II was the Atlantic Charter signed by Franklin Roosevelt and Churchill "somewhere in the Atlantic" four months before Pearl Harbor. Point Two of the Charter bound the Western Alliance to "no territorial changes that do not accord with the freely expressed wishes of the peoples concerned." Point Three — most important of the eight statements of purpose — promised "sovereign rights and self-government restored to those who have been forcibly deprived of them." These points were violated repeatedly by the West as it tried to suppress nationalist revolutions in Madagascar (1943-44), Greece (1944), Algeria, Tunisia, Morocco (1945), Indochina and Indonesia (1945-46) — all of them *before* the Soviets had begun to renege on pledges of elections in Poland, and after it had become obvious that a modus vivendi with the West was unlikely.

Whatever the rights and wrongs of the Cold War, however, many prominent Americans recognized that the "communist threat" of the 1940s was not one of military invasion but of encouraging nationalist revolutions — if and when Stalin decided to do so. John Foster Dulles, for instance, conceded in March 1949 that the Soviet government "does not contemplate the use of war as an instrument of its national policy. I do not know any responsible official, military or civilian, in this government or any government, who believes that the Soviet government now plans conquest by open military aggression."

David Horowitz has assembled a half dozen similar statements by leading figures. James Forrestal recorded in his diary June 10, 1946, that he thought the Russians "would not move this summer — in fact, at any time." General Walter Bedell Smith on August 3, 1948, two months after the Berlin blockade, advised the War Council "that the Russians do not want war." His successor, Admiral Alan G. Kirk, was reported by *U.S. News and World Report* six months after the onset of the Korean War, as seeing "no signs in Moscow that Russia expects war now. . . . Currently Admiral Kirk detects none of the telltale signs of war that the experts watch for." Reminiscing on the early Cold War period in May 1965, George Kennan reinforced the Dulles estimate: "It was perfectly clear to anyone with even a rudimentary knowledge of the Russia of that day that the Soviet leaders had no intention of attempting to advance their cause by launching military attacks with their own armed forces across frontiers."[14]

General Douglas MacArthur — no dove — said in mid-1957: "Our government has kept us in a perpetual state of fear — kept us in a continuous stampede of patriotic fervor — with the cry of a grave national emergency. . . . Yet, in retrospect, these disasters seem never to have happened, seem never to have been real." Even President Nixon raised a few eyebrows early in his administration by referring to the Soviet Union's military stance as "defensive," rather than offensive.

The United States, it seems clear, backed itself into the military-industrial stall not out of fear of Soviet invasion, but out of other motives. This does not mean that the misgivings of American citizens over purges and authoritarianism in the Soviet orbit was disingenuous or synthetic. It wasn't; many alarming things were taking place in Stalin's domain. But the men at the levers of power in America interpreted the word defense quite differently from its traditional meaning. Historian William Appleman Williams quotes congressmen at the end of the war who felt that the nation's purpose must be to seek "world power as a trustee for civilization." Henry B. Luce, publisher of *Time*, called this the "American century," and business spokesmen referred to the American role as "missionaries of capitalism and democracy," presumably equating the two.[15]

Most forthright of all perhaps was Undersecretary of State Dean Acheson, who told a congressional committee in 1944 that "it is a problem of markets. . . . We have got to see that what the country produces is used and is sold under financial arrangements which make its production possible." Under a different system, he admitted, "you could use the entire production of the country in the United States," but under our present form of free enterprise, the Government "must look to foreign markets." If it didn't "it seems clear that we are in for a very bad time . . . having the most far-reaching consequences upon our economic and social system."[16] America's goal in the postwar world, it seems, was not quite as eleemosynary as its public proclamations pretended; a dollar sign lurked in the shadows.

Shortly after Harry Truman became President, he told a visitor, according to Williams, "that the Russians would soon be put in their places; and that the United States would then take the lead in running the world in a way that the world ought to be run." In a March 1947 speech at Baylor University that has never received the attention it deserved, Truman argued that freedom was more urgent than peace, and that in the final analysis it could be assured only through the worldwide prevalence of "free enterprise." Freedom — of enterprise, speech, worship, assembly, all interdependent on each other — could not exist where the Government does the planning and operates foreign trade. The enemy of free enterprise was "regimented economies," and "unless we act, and act decisively," said Truman, those regimented economies would become "the pattern of the next century." To guard against the danger he urged that "the whole world should adopt the American system." That system "could survive in America only *if it became a world system.*" (Italics added.)[17]

Here in defensive rhetoric Truman was explaining what it was about communism that threatened us — making it necessary to "act decisively." Certainly its military machine posed a challenge, though as Dulles, Forrestal, and others clearly understood, it was not a decisive one. What concerned Truman and the military men who ran his State Department, was the issue of "free" versus "regimented" economies. The Soviet orbit's own economy was "regimented," and if the new nations — whose revolutions were supported by the Soviets — were to become similarly "regimented," American free enterprise would find a large area of the world closed off to its trade and investment, as well as its needs in raw materials. Early in the century the United States had been relatively self-sufficient and had a small overage of raw materials for export; but by midcentury it was using 35 to 40 percent of the free world's supply of basic commodities for which it paid $5 to $6 billion a year.[18] To guarantee markets and supplies a new strategy was needed therefore — economic, political, and military — to make the American system a world system.

The military-industrial complex advanced inexorably to further this purpose — what Prof. Neal D. Houghton calls "global imperialism," by contrast with the "continental imperialism" the United States practiced in the nineteenth century when it expanded westward, and the episodic imperialism, say in Latin America, of the early part of this century.[19] The traditional form of imperialism — the naked occupation of foreign lands — was no longer feasible or desirable at the end of World War II. But other means were at hand, and it was these that the military-industrial complex put into magnificent practice to defend and extend the free enterprise system against the regimented ones.

Though Americans find it hard to believe of their own country, history has punctuated — both positively and negatively — the cause-and-effect relationship between military forces and bases overseas, on the one hand, and economic empire on the other. When Winston Churchill promoted the military intervention of 14 foreign armies on Soviet soil from 1918 to 1920, it was on the theory that the example of bolshevism would accelerate revolution and destroy England's *colonial empire*. "We may well be," he wrote Lloyd George, "within measurable distance of universal collapse and anarchy throughout Europe and Asia." If the empire was to be saved "the baby [bolshevism] must be strangled in its crib."[20] A State Department memorandum of December 10, 1940, pointed out that if Japan should drive our ally, Britain, out of the Far East "our general diplomatic and strategic position would be considerably weakened — by our loss of Chinese, Indian, and South Seas markets (and our loss of much of the Japanese market for our goods as Japan became more and more self-sufficient) as well as by the insurmountable restrictions upon our access to the rubber, tin, jute, and other vital materials of the Asian and oceanic regions."[21] Taiwan, which was saved for Chiang Kai-shek by American arms, listed some 500 American manufacturers in its territory as of 1966, according to Prof. John M. Swomley, Jr. — and sheltered about 50,000 American troops. Japan, militarily ruled by the United States in the postwar period, was America's second largest trading partner after Canada, still had a garrison of 40,000 U.S. soldiers at the end of 1965 — and $676 million of private U.S. investments.[22] That this relationship between military power and economic gain is not secret to American businessmen is evidenced by this statement of Henry M. Sperry, vice-president of the First National City Bank:

> We believe that we're going to win this war [in Vietnam]. Afterwards you'll have a major job of reconstruction on your hands. That will take financing and financing means banks. . . . It would be illogical to permit the English and French to monopolize the banking business because South Vietnam's economy is becoming more and more United States oriented."[23]

In theory American efficiency and American dollar surpluses (the government poured $175 billion into procurement during the war, including $25 billion in plants and equipment loaned to private corporations) should have made it possible to penetrate the world market with little difficulty. But in actual fact other nations usually put up barriers such as tariffs, quotas, or denial of the right to repatriate profits, that keep their doors totally or partly shut to foreign exports and investments. It was these closed doors that the military-industrial complex had to pry open in dozens of countries.

An insight into how it is done can perhaps be gleaned from recent developments in Thailand, which calls itself appropriately the gateway of Southeast Asia. Since 1947, when a democratic civilian government was overthrown by a "Siamese Caesar" who had collaborated with the Japanese in World War II, this pleasant land has been under the heels of military dictators. Its government showed certain trends toward state control of the economy, until it ran into difficulties with dissenters and, later, guerrillas. To secure its internal position the regime, now headed by General Thanom Kittikachorn, called on the United States for help, and was rewarded from 1961 to 1967 with $640 million, about two thirds of it military aid.

In return, the Siamese government not only granted the United States military bases and airfields from which to bomb Vietnam, but a host of concessions for American industry. It provided tax holidays, guarantees against nationalization, and guarantees that profits can be repatriated and capital transferred without hindrance.

With this kind of encouragement American investment has increased to $195 million, with considerably more on the way. Since the annual GNP of Thailand is less than $4 billion this is no small stake. Caltex, Esso, Firestone Rubber, the Chase Manhattan Bank, IBM, Bank of America, and Kaiser Aluminum have all gained a modest foothold in the economy. Standard of Indiana has built a $35 million refinery, Union Carbide is mining tin, Goodyear has constructed three tire factories, and a number of American banks have opened branches in the country.[24]

Another nation in the process of being "Americanized" is the incredibly rich Indonesia. (President Eisenhower asked in 1953: "If we lost Vietnam and Malaya, how would we, the free world, hold the rich empire of Indonesia?") After the coup d'etat against Sukarno and the bloodbath of hundreds of thousands of "Communists" in 1966, the United States offered various forms of aid to President Suharto. Within a half year the government proved its pliability to foreign investment. Property expropriated by the previous regime was returned to its former owners, and a law was promulgated which virtually relieves new outside investors of taxation, and pledges — as Suharto explains it — that Indonesia will "never . . . interfere in the affairs of private business organization" — a sharp reversal from Sukarno's policies.

The U.S. does not as yet have military bases in Indonesia and there are still some onerous restrictions on foreign investments, such as the 65 percent royalty on net returns. But the door has been pried ajar a little: American Freeport Sulphur is investing $76.5 million in a copper mine, oil companies are negotiating to exploit the country's petroleum deposits, and 15 American banks have been authorized to establish branches. Of the $330 million in foreign investments approved as of mid-1968 (the target is $2.5 billion within five years) American firms or their subsidiaries in Canada and South Korea own almost two thirds.

An apt summary of the policy sponsored by the military-industrial complex is provided by Dr. Herbert I. Schiller, editor of *The Quarterly Review of Economics and Business:*

> The association of the objectives of American expansionism with the concept of freedom, in which the former are obscured and the latter is emphasized, has been a brilliant achievement in American policy. Rarely has the word "freedom" produced so much confusion and obtained so much misdirected endorsement.

"Americans," echos Harvard political science professor Samuel P. Huntington, "devoted much attention to the expansion of communism (which, in fact, expanded very little after 1949), and in the process they tended to ignore the expansion of the United States influence and presence throughout much of the world."[25]

To "open the door" — whether in Europe, Asia, Africa, or

Latin America — the military-industrial complex relies primarily on two techniques:

1. A system of aid and loans aimed at stabilizing the economies of our allies, but also at keeping them moored to the "American way."

2. A system of military alliances, military training and support, as well as use of the CIA and AFL-CIO labor leaders, to assure that the governments we consider friendly remain in power.

Despite a general belief to the contrary, American aid, both economic and military, has conditions attached to it. The Marshall Plan, for instance, provided among other things that European nations would permit American investments to enter their home and colonial market *on an equal basis* with themselves.[26] Under this spur, direct American investments in Europe have zoomed to $16 billion. Today a third of all European autos are manufactured by U.S. firms, a quarter to a third of the oil industry in the Common Market is in American hands. American corporations in Britain produce 10 percent of its manufactures and account for 17 percent of its exports. "Western Europe," wrote correspondent Joseph C. Harsch, a couple of years ago, "is today more disturbed about American economic power than Russian military power."[27]

Conditions imposed on Latin America for military and economic aid are designed to effectively tie the southern republics to the North American chariot. Formally, the United States requires that in return for low-interest loans (70 to 80 percent of Alliance for Progress "aid" is in the form of loans, not grants) the recipient state must earmark half or more for purchase of equipment from the United States, must ship half of these purchases in American bottoms, and must agree not to nationalize American firms without "fair" payment. Further, it must satisfy Washington as to the "soundness" of its budget and must import an equivalent amount of goods from the States. Informally, the loans are wielded to win concessions for American firms. For almost three years the U.S., for instance, cut aid to the bone for Peru because it did not come to terms with a Standard Oil subsidiary. The Goulart regime in Brazil, leaning toward neutralism, received only a dribble of aid, but the regime headed by General Castelo Branco, which overthrew him, was lavished with $234.8 million in the first year. Perhaps the reason was that Castelo's planning minister, Roberto Campos, openly proclaimed that the only way to develop Brazil was by inviting hundreds of millions of private investments from North America.

Eugene Black, former president of the World Bank and later President Johnson's advisor on Asian development, summed up the advantages of foreign aid to U.S. business, thus:

The three major benefits are: (1) foreign aid provides a substantial and immediate market for U.S. goods and services; (2) foreign aid stimulates the development of new overseas markets for U.S. companies; (3) foreign aid orients national economies toward a free enterprise system in which U.S. firms can prosper.[28]

The proof of the pudding is in the eating. American investments abroad have pyramided from $11.8 billion in 1950 to $54.6 billion in 1966 and continue to rise at $4 to $6 billion a year. They were $66 billion at the end of 1968, resulting in an output of goods estimated at $200 billion — or more than six times the $33 billion exported from the U.S. proper. A study by the International Chamber of Commerce showed that 77 of the ,500 largest U.S. manufacturers were doing more than a quarter of their business in overseas plants.[29] That all this was highly lucrative is indicated by what has been happening in Latin America. From 1950 to 1965 U.S. corporate investments there rose from $4.5 billion to $10.3 billion; in the same period profits transferred home — in addition to what was left behind for additional investment — was $11.3 billion.[30] Following a similar boom pattern, U.S. exports climbed from $4 billion in 1940 to $10.5 billion in 1945 and $33 billion in 1968. Even allowing for the decline in the value of money, this global expansion is sensational.

It would be wrong to say that individual American firms treat local populations worse than native business does. On the contrary the U.S. corporations usually pay higher wages and provide more social benefits for the workers they employ. There is no comparing, for instance, the wages paid by Jersey Standard

(Creole) in Venezuela with what a Venezuelan manufacturer pays his hired hands. The trouble is that the U.S. firms are interested primarily in their own profits rather than the development of the countries in which they do business, and this tends to warp native progress. By way of example, before 1939 foreign oil companies in Mexico sold most of their petroleum abroad and repatriated most of their profits to New York. The nationalized agency, Pemex, that took over these holdings, by contrast, used the oil to develop the *Mexican* economy. Oil was used to further electrification, and through electrification a host of manufacturing industries. Oil and natural gas today provide 90 percent of the nation's energy. "By supplying fuel below cost," writes the First National City Bank of New York, "Pemex has played an important role in subsidizing agriculture, industry, and public transport."[31] Moreover, it is to the interest of the U.S. corporations to ally themselves with conservative elements in the native country, because the conservatives are much more likely to give them favorable terms for conducting their business. To the extent that such men hold government reins social reform is inhibited and the plight of the native lower classes remains stagnant or grows worse. After the CIA-sponsored overthrow of Jacobo Arbenz in Guatemala, for instance, U.S. private investment spurted sensationally. But a recent report — 15 years later — of social conditions shows that three quarters of the people live on what the U.N. considers a "below starvation level," three quarters are illiterate, four fifths lack adequate drinking-water facilities or toilets, one fifth of the children die before they reach the age of five.[32]

Nevertheless, it is conservative leadership abroad that the military-industrial complex generally curries for its policy of global expansion. To assure that the expansion continues, Washington relies not only on economic aid but on military measures to guarantee that American allies do not fall prey to the tempest of revolution.

For example, military aid of $50 to $100 million a year ($1.1 billion from 1953 to 1966), has been supplied to Latin America even though, as former Defense Secretary McNamara conceded in June 1963, there is no "threat of significant overt external aggression." The weapons and the training of thousands of Latin American officers in counterinsurgency at such places as Fort Gulick in Panama or Fort McNair in Washington, goes to improve "internal security capabilities." Miguel Ydigoras, former president of Guatemala who was himself jettisoned by a military coup in 1963, says of military aid that "generally speaking, modern weapons are not used by the military to defend the territorial integrity of their respective countries, but to repress popular aspirations and undermine democratic institutions."

That the Pentagon is no shy outsider looking in, but a decisive overseer in this process can be gauged from this sentence in a memo of the U.S. embassy in Chile: "The United States Army and the United States Air Force missions are located in the Chilean Ministry of Defense building in Santiago, with the United States Naval mission located in Viña del Mar." Though they also have contingents at the embassies, a good part of Uncle Sam's military missions work out of the command posts of the native government. They are privy to all secrets and, usually, to plans for coups d'etat.

Whatever notions the American people have of "preserving peace," the American military is not coy in stating the purposes of its Latin American work. General Robert W. Porter, Jr., who heads the Southern Command at Balboa in the Canal Zone says:

> Latin America is one of our largest trading partners — $7 billion in 1967 — and after Canada and Western Europe, the largest area for United States private investments now totaling almost $13 billion. During and since World War II, Latin America has been a major United States supplier of approximately 30 strategic materials, including copper, tin, and petroleum.

The counterinsurgents being trained, therefore, are needed to act "in conjunction with the police and other security forces . . . to control disorders and riots," and discourage "those elements which are tempted to resort to violence to overthrow the government." Without American guns and training the Bosch government could not have been overthrown by Dominican militarists in 1963, the Bolivian government by General René Barrientos, the Brazilian government by General Castelo Branco, and so forth and so on.[33] "Arms are used in Latin America," comments *The New York Times,* "solely to maintain internal security which would be legitimate except for the fact that the military keep themselves in relative luxury and hold the ultimate power in their hands to make and unmake governments."[34]

Without the American military, Taiwan would long ago have fallen back to China, for it is the American Seventh Fleet which patrols the waters between Taiwan and the mainland that keeps it sovereign. Nations like Saudi Arabia, Jordan, and most of Latin America would long ago have succumbed to internal revolt. Two or three billion dollars of American aid helped France defend its empire in Indochina (though not well), and NATO arms supplied by Washington were used by France in a vain effort to defeat the Algerian guerrillas. Chiang Kai-shek was given $3 billion to hold off the Communists in China. The Shah of Iran was reinvested with power through the machinations of the CIA, with American guns.

From 1949 to mid-1966 the Pentagon sold $16 billion of weaponry and gave away $30 billion more to foreign governments aligned with us. The chief advantage of these grants and sales, as Amaury de Riencourt has observed, "lies in binding to the Pentagon satellite military establishments in Latin America, the Far East, and Europe. . ." All in all, he says, the United States has assumed a "protectorate" over "more than 40 nations covering some 15 million square miles with populations amounting to over 600 million human beings."[35] With the wink of an eye the Pentagon is often able to induce satellite military establishments in these "protectorates" to overthrow governments hostile to the American system. It is no longer necessary — except in extreme cases like Vietnam or the Dominican Republic — to *occupy* a country to bring it into a great power's sphere of influence. The same result can be achieved through aid, loans, military support, and satellite armies.

The satellite armies are an adjunct to the American empire, and in many ways preferable to U.S. troops. "Military assistance," McNamara told the Foreign Relations Committee in 1966, "provides essential arms, training, and related support to five million men in allied and other friendly forces. . . . These men are critical to our forward strategy." He boasted that while it cost $4,500 to maintain a U.S. soldier, the five million foreign troops "critical to our forward strategy" along the periphery of China and the Soviet Union can be supported on $540 a year. "We get eight soldiers to one for our money," is the cynical comment of former Senator Joseph Clark.[36]

The military-industrial complex, it is clear, was born out of motives more earthy than its sponsors imply. If its function is to "preserve the peace," its definition of the word peace is synonymous with global expansion. Many decades ago Lord Cecil Rhodes, who conquered much of Africa for the British, suggested that the simplest way to achieve peace was for England to convert the rest of the world to its colony. If the same thought hasn't occurred to the American military-industrial complex in the present period, it is at least there subliminally.

CHAPTER THREE

Internal Imperialism

Back in 1782 Colonel Lewis Nicola and a group of officers proposed to General George Washington that he lead an Army revolt to establish a monarchy in the United States, with himself as king. The general turned down the offer. But when officers, a year later, asked him to become president of the Society of the Cincinnati, formed by Major General Henry Knox and Baron von Steuben to honor the men who had fought in the war, he gratefully accepted. Until it became the focus of bitter criticism by the leaders of the American revolution, Washington saw nothing wrong with it. But one after another — Jefferson, Sam Adams, John Adams, Elbridge Gerry, John Jay — denounced the Cincinnati as inimical to democracy, especially in planning a role for military men in politics and in the hereditary features of membership. In Massachusetts the General Court passed resolutions condemning the Cincinnati, and in Rhode Island and North Carolina movements sprang up to deny any member of the Society the right to vote or hold office — on the theory that a politicalized officer caste endangered liberty and equality. Aedanus Burke, one of the chief justices in South Carolina, expressed the widely-shared view "that military commanders acquiring fame, and accustomed to receive the obedience of armies, are generally in their hearts aristocrats, and enemies of the popular equality of a republic."[1]

Many military heroes were to be elected President in the ensuing years, but the military as such has never been permitted until recently to play a role in political affairs. It was to lead armies and operate navies, nothing else. This stern division between civilian prerogatives and military prerogatives is one reason, perhaps, why there has never been anything approaching a coup d'etat in the United States. Law and tradition decreed that the armed services be subordinate to civilian rule and keep their fingers out of politics. This was in accord with the underlying thesis of a democracy that the people must retain the power to correct their government when it is wrong. To permit the military to dabble in politics — with its discipline, its fame, its hand on the gun — posed the danger that it would gain a dominant hold over the Executive, Congress, and the economy that no popular force could restrain or control.

The present military-industrial complex has upset these principles and traditions, threatening the nation with a political monopoly many times more ominous than economic monopolies. If global expansion brings us repeatedly to the brink of war, the domestic effect of militarism drives us toward the monolithic state. For if there is one thing that stands out in the military-industrial complex it is a trend to what may be called — for want of a better term — "internal imperialism." Its influence penetrates, as Eisenhower said in his famous warning of January 17, 1961, "every city, every state house, every office of the federal government." It creates pockets of support in scores of milieus, from Congress to the Boy Scouts, from trade associations to labor unions, from academia to the church. And it holds these forces together with mountains of money, promotions for the officer caste, appeals to patriotism, and a rabid anti-communism which it wields, in the words of former Marine Corps Commandant General David M. Shoup (retired), "somewhat like a religion."

In 1962 Fletcher Knebel and Charles W. Bailey II wrote a novel, *Seven Days in May,* in which the Joint Chiefs of Staff prepared to kidnap the President and take over the government because the chief executive had signed a nuclear disarmament treaty with the Soviets. The Knebel-Bailey book was good fiction, but overdrawn politics, for the military-industrial complex does not have to arrange anything so drastic as a coup d'etat. It need only insinuate itself into enough institutions to become an unchallengeable political monopoly, to achieve the same purpose.

The military, as already noted, tried during World War II to gain control over the American economy. It didn't succeed, due to Franklin Roosevelt's resistance, but it didn't entirely fail, either. When hostilities ended the officer class was ensconced in a number of important government posts relating to industry. Colonel John R. Alison was appointed Assistant Secretary of Commerce for Aeronautics, Major General Philip B. Fleming became head of the Federal Works Agency and director of the Office of Temporary Controls, Vice Admiral William W. Smith was appointed chairman of the Maritime Commission, Major General Robert M. Littlejohn of the War Assets Administration, General Graves B. Erskine, chief of the Retraining and Re-employment Administration. "There were scores of lesser fry in lesser posts and missions," commented *Time* (January 20, 1947).

After the war, the military tried its hardest to assert sovereignty over the nation's youth and its foreign service. Except for the Civil War and World Wars I and II, the United States had never conscripted men into the armed forces — and never in peace times. From 1944 to 1955, however, the generals mounted a campaign for universal military training (UMT) more far-reaching than the wartime draft. Service in the armed forces would no longer be *selective*, with men deferred for a variety of reasons, but *total* — all youth reaching the age of eighteen, except the physically handicapped, would be required to take military training for a period of years and then placed in the reserves to continue their training a few nights each month and every summer. Many congressmen and senators could not understand why we needed so many troops, when we had atom bombs that could kill 75,000 people at one fell blow. But as Major General F. O. Bowman, a commander at Fort Knox, explained later, there was more than military needs involved: "We have these young men while they are young and fresh. Their minds have not been cluttered up by worldliness. They make wonderful subjects for Army training." Presumably civilian schools did not offer youth the right approach to citizenship, for Assistant Secretary of Defense Anna Rosenberg explained in 1952 that "a large part of the training as envisaged . . . is citizenship training, literary training, training in morale, and training in the type of things that young people ought to have."[2] The military's own idea of good citizenship is attested to by the armed forces security questionnaire which draftees are required to fill out to prove they are "reliable, trustworthy, of good character, and of complete unswerving loyalty to the United States." They are asked to state whether they are now or have ever been members of any one of 300 organizations on the Attorney General's subversive list, including of course the Communist Party, and such esoteric and dangerous groups as People's Drama, Inc. and the Chopin Cultural Center.

The military did not win its war for UMT; it had to settle for second best, *selective* service. But it mounted a propaganda drive on its behalf such as the nation had never seen before and which a congressional committee branded as an outright violation of "section 201, title 18 of the United States Code." The committee, headed by Congressman Forrest A. Harness, found "that the War Department is using government funds in an improper manner for propaganda purposes." The propaganda, moreover, "followed a pattern unworthy of any department of government." An outline for "veterans' radio panels," prepared by the War Department, virtually labeled anyone who opposed UMT as a subversive or a moron: "The opposition to universal military training," it said, "is generally not based on fact but rather on such generalizations as democracy, morals, aggression, education, and pacifism. The chief opponents are parents, church groups, educators, subversive groups, and a large section of the public which does not think."[3] In the 1948 campaign for UMT the War Department enlisted the support of 370 national organizations "including the U.S. Chamber of Commerce and the American Legion; it . . . contacted 351 mayors in the principal cities of the land; it . . . promoted at least 591 articles and editorials in the press." The Boy Scouts were prevailed on to distribute fact sheets and the American Legion was induced to print 600,000 copies of a brochure titled "You and the Army Reserve."[4] Assistant Secretary of War, Howard C. Peterson, frankly conceded that government money was being used for propaganda "to sell the program to the public with the hope that the public would sell it to Congress." To prove the need for UMT, the generals issued releases and gave interviews pointing to the horrible incineration that would occur from an atom bomb attack on the U.S. — before the Russians had tested a single bomb — and to the imminent danger of war.

If the military had to settle for a partial victory in controlling the nation's youth, the draft has nonetheless been pivotal both to its power and plans. Prof. John M. Swomley, Jr. wrote in March 1967:

> It is the draft which makes it possible for the President to send 400,000 troops into Vietnam without a declaration of war. Each step of escalation was possible only because the Joint Chiefs of Staff and the President knew they could draw on hundreds of thousands of American youth without going to Congress for such authority. If the President had had to ask Congress either for a draft or a declaration of war he would have faced a national debate over his policies. It is also true that the United States could not bypass the United Nations and act as the world's policeman if it were not for the draft. Without an inflated Army based on peacetime conscription it would be impossible to maintain garrisons all over the world.[5]

A second field for military infiltration into civilian politics, and of course a decisive one, has been the foreign services. At first the penetration was simple and direct. "Today," boasted the *Army and Navy Bulletin* of January 18, 1947, "the Army has virtual control of foreign affairs. . . . The chain of control in diplomatic hot spots, both in the execution of basic policy and in the formulation of ad hoc arrangements, lies almost totally in the hands of the military authorities." Few people objected when the military architects of victory were placed in the civilian saddle for international affairs. General Douglas MacArthur ruled Japan, Lieutenant General Lucius D. Clay ruled the American sector of Germany, and Lieutenant General Geoffrey Keyes the American sector of Austria. It didn't seem amiss therefore to turn over the State Department to the military. Thus, General of the Army George C. Marshall was appointed Secretary of State, and ten of the 20 executive officers in the department were transferees from the military services. Brigadier General Charles E. Saltzman served as Assistant Secretary for Occupied Areas, having succeeded General John M. Hildring, who "brought with him to the State Department 26 of his assistants in the War Department. John E. Peurifoy, another assistant secretary, had graduated from Deputy Assistant Secretary of the Combined Chiefs of Staff. Undersecretary Robert A. Lovett had held the post of Assistant Secretary of War around the time of World War II. Lieutenant General Walter Bedell Smith was ambassador to Moscow, Admiral Alan G. Kirk ambassador to Belgium, and Lieutenant General Albert C. Wedemeyer was assigned to head a special mission to China. The generals and admirals, in due course, departed from State, but their influence on foreign affairs is guaranteed in another manner. Under the National Security Act of 1947 they play a formal role, through the National Security Council, in advising the President on international policy. When a senator asked George Marshall in May 1951 whose side the President took in disputes between State and DOD, he replied: "I can recall no occasion where Mr. Truman has acted adversely to the Chiefs of Staff and the Secretary of Defense in relation to the State Department."[6] Anyway, all the postwar secretaries of state, and especially Acheson, Dulles, and Rusk, have been closely identified with the military-industrial complex by background and ideology.

As a footnote to the military's incursion into politics it might be worth adding that as of 1953 nine Army generals and 58 colonels, on leave or retired, were working for civilian agencies of government; and as of 1957, 200 generals and admirals, plus 1,300 colonels or Navy officers of similar rank and 6,000 of lower grade. Recent figures are not available but they are doubtless substantial.

The zest for expansion, for sewing up a pocket of influence, has been the distinguishing feature of the armed services. All bureaucracies of course have a similar proclivity, but the Pentagon has been many times blessed. It had the adulation of the people for having won the war. It had a convenient enemy to lay before the public constantly — communism. It could conjure up images of impending horrors by mysterious weapons no one had ever seen or could question. It was buoyed by a more than average ambition, not for profit admittedly, but for power and prestige. And it was fortunate, above all, in having many potential allies in civilian places, who for reasons of "pork or patriotism" were more papist than the pope.

Out of this confluence of interests has evolved a refashioned power elite in America, more formidable than any ever known before. At the base of the military-industrial complex pyramid, naturally, is the Pentagon itself, the fountainhead, though not the brainpower of the complex. Above the base, not necessarily in the order of importance are:

1. A civilian-militarist faction in the Congress.

2. The large corporate contractors who do business with the Pentagon, a sort of Who's Who of American industry.

3. A selected group of organizations that act as liaison between industry and the military, such as the American Ordnance Association or the National Security Industrial Association.

4. Sixteen DOD-subsidized research organizations popularly called "think-tanks," such as Rand Corporation, and the Institute for Defense Analysis (until recently a consortium of 12 universities). These are headed for the most part by former defense officials: H. S. Rowen, president of Rand, was formerly Deputy Assistant Secretary of Defense; General Maxwell D. Taylor, president of IDA, was at one time chairman of the Joint Chiefs of Staff. The purpose of the think-tanks is to research knotty problems in a host of areas, including the social sciences, and to formulate strategic principles for the Pentagon.

5. A considerable number of private research and educational organizations, such as the Hoover Institution on War, Revolution, and Peace; the American Security Council, the Center for Strategic Studies, the American Enterprise Institute for Public Policy Research.

6. The leadership of the AFL-CIO, especially the international affairs department headed by Jay Lovestone; as well as a number of satellite organizations — e.g. the American Institute for Free Labor Development — whose operations it controls.

7. The academic community whose fate is tied to the Pentagon, including such prominent professors as Edward Teller, such schools as the Massachusetts Institute of Technology (MIT) and Johns Hopkins, and the "contract centers" run by elite universities.

These seven categories might be called the active sector of the military-industrial complex. There are also some passive forces that play a part: the veterans organizations (there were 23 million veterans in the country as of 1968 or one out of every five adults), the trade associations and chambers of commerce, the fundamentalist wing of the church (the Rev. Billy Graham, the late Cardinal Spellman, the military chaplains), sections of the mass media *(Chicago Tribune, New York Daily News)*, and scores of individual correspondents and commentators.

The individuals who guide the destinies of the military-industrial complex are a select group who know each other well and who tend to shuttle back and forth from one milieu to another. General Lauris Norstad, former Supreme Allied Commander in Europe, becomes president of Owens-Corning Fiberglas; Admiral William M. Fechteler, after retiring as chief of naval operations, becomes a consultant to a division of General Electric; Admiral Arleigh Burke, another chief of naval operations, becomes a director of many corporations and head of a think-tank at Georgetown University.

On the other hand, industrial, legal, and academic figures shift from private industry to key posts at the Pentagon. The first Secretary of Defense, James V. Forrestal, was a former president of the Dillon, Read investment firm; Secretary Charles E. Wilson made the changeover from General Motors (he is not to be confused with the Charles E. Wilson at General Electric); Neil H. McElroy from Procter and Gamble; Robert S. McNamara from Ford; Clark Clifford from a law firm which included Du Pont, RCA, General Electric, and Phillips Petroleum as clients. All three Pentagon directors of Defense Research and Engineering, Herbert F. York, Harold Brown, and John S. Foster, Jr., came to their posts from the Livermore Laboratory at the University of California.

David Packard, deputy secretary and the richest man ever to serve in this post, was the co-founder of Hewlett-Packard, a Palo Alto electronics and computer firm which did more than $100 million of government work in 1968. Willis Hawkins, vice-president of Lockheed, later turned his talents to the Army as assistant secretary for research and development. Scientists and engineers by the thousand find themselves moving from the pay-roll of industry to government and back again, usually working on the same weapons system.

These are all men of power, and their power in the end gains political sanction from Congress. Without a prevailing voice in Congress, comparable to the one it has in the Executive branch of government, the military-industrial complex would be like a bird with one wing. Fortunately for the complex it has a built-in constituency on Capitol Hill. According to a tally made by William McGaffin and Robert Gruenberg of the *Chicago Daily News*, 100 of the 435 representatives and 30 of the 100 senators carry officer ranks — active, inactive, and retired — in the military forces.[7] Two members of the Senate Armed Services Committee, Democrat Howard Cannon of Nevada and Republican Strom Thurmond of South Carolina, are major generals and one other, Republican Jack Miller of Iowa, is a brigadier general. Representative Robert Sikes of Florida, a leading Democrat on the Military Appropriations Committee, who usually writes its military construction bills, is also a major general of the Army reserve. Not all the 130 legislators wearing military hats are hawks (e.g. Senator Stephen Young of Ohio, a lieutenant colonel in the reserves, is distinctly dovish) but the vast majority are, and some of them not accidentally so. One congressman told McGaffin and Gruenberg that when he was appointed a member of the Armed Services Committee the Army "offered to make me a colonel" even though he had never risen above corporal in the regular services.

Add to the 100 congressmen in the military reserves the 61 who own stock in the top 100 defense companies, and, even with some overlap, you have a formidable force predisposed to the militarist view before any issue is debated.[8] Four of these shareholders are on the key Armed Services Committee and five on the Joint Committee on Defense Production. No one knows how many senators have a similar stake in the weapons business, because they are not required to make such disclosures, but there must be some.

The Pentagon woos Congress as ardently as Romeo wooed Juliet. It employs 339 lobbyists to plead its case, inform the legislators about contracts in their districts, process inquiries about boys in the armed services, and perform a host of other duties. At the end of World War II there were only five such legislative agents.[9] To get some idea of the dimensions of this political activity in Congress: the largest private lobbying force in 1967 was the Postal Clerks Union which spent $277,524; DOD had $4.1 million budgeted for that purpose, presumably in addition to salaries, and of course in addition to the lobbying done on its behalf by defense contractors and associations.

Legislators friendly to the cause are given free airplane trips — sometimes just to a football game — and are wined and dined like potentates from the Mideast, all at taxpayers' expense. When Senator Richard B. Russell (Dem.-Ga.), chairman of the Appropriations Committee, wanted to go to a convention not too long ago the Air Force generously flew him there in a VIP jet. While there he received an urgent message from Senator Mansfield that an important vote was coming up. The Air Force flew him back 2,000 miles to Washington, with a colonel acting as host, a chef broiling steaks, and a bartender serving drinks.[10]

One night in March 1969 an "appreciation dinner" was held for Senator John Stennis (Dem.-Miss.) in Jackson, Mississippi, to memorialize the fact that he had risen to Russell's former post as chairman of the Armed Services Committee. Most of the top brass were flown in on government planes to celebrate the occasion, including Defense Secretary Laird, four of the five members of the Joint Chiefs of Staff, the Navy Secretary, and many others. For entertainment the Pentagon flew in a naval choir from Pensacola, Florida, and an Army WAC band from Fort McClellan, Alabama. The 1,300 guests thought it was a grand party, even if the U.S. government had to pay much of the bill.

Russell and Stennis, properly, rate high in the Pentagon's firmament of friends, as do their counterparts in the House, George D. Mahon (Dem.-Tex.) and L. Mendel Rivers (Dem.-S.C.). The four men head appropriations and armed services committees which, as Seymour Hersh points out, are little more than "conduits" for translating Pentagon wishes into legislation. Russell says:

> There is no hesitation in my mind in stating that we cannot continue to support a war, be capable of honoring our commitments abroad, and maintain an adequate defense posture, without increasing the size of our defense budget in the near future. As reluctant as Congress will be to accept that statement, I make it unequivocally and without fear of contradition.[11]

This is the kind of talk the military-industrial complex likes to hear. Rivers says the same sort of thing more crudely but more forcefully: "The Navy is obsolete. It needs at least $100 billion to be brought up to where it ought to be."[12] On the Vietnam War he is sure that any competent general, if allowed to fight in the "true military fashion . . . wouldn't take over four weeks" to win it. All four committee chairmen are Southerners, conservatives, and aging — Russell is 71, Stennis 67, Mahon 68, and Rivers 63. The hearings they hold on military matters, usually secret, seldom call on experts opposed to the military view. No one opposed to ABM, for instance, testified before Russell's committee; a year ago both Mahon and Russell candidly acknowledged that they hadn't called a single witness on extensive military budget hearings except those from the administration. Hearings on the nuclear test ban before the Senate Armed Services Committee in 1963 were converted into a cavalcade of Air Force officers testifying *against* the ban — even though the administration favored it. Little wonder then that the irreverent call this committee "the ratifying arm of the Joint Chiefs of Staff." The Joint Chiefs reward friends such as these, not only with airplane rides, but more enduring benefits.

The most sought-after rewards, as might be expected, are defense contracts or military installations in the legislator's bailiwick. The closest friends in Congress, such as the four key committee chairmen, of course, get the plums. "When you read the requests for military construction," Congressman Jamie L. Whitten (Dem.-Miss.) said some years ago, "they had them listed by states so you could see every member had a monetary interest in passage."[13] Moreover, "you can look at some of our key people in the key places in Congress and go see how many military establishments are in their districts." When another Air Force base was proposed for Russell's state of Georgia a few years back a general wryly remarked that "one more base would sink the state." Though it is relatively small — twenty-first in area, sixteenth in population — it commands a DOD payroll for military and civilian personnel, of more than $900 million a year, fourth in the nation behind California ($2.5 billion), Texas ($1.6 billion), and Virginia ($1.2 billion), as of fiscal 1967.[14] When the award was made for the C-5A cargo planes — more than $3 billion, but expected to run over $5 billion — it was not surprising that it went to Lockheed in Marietta, *Georgia*. Lockheed's payroll of $200 million a year to 26,000 workers makes it the largest industrial employer in the state.

Congressman Rivers, with unabashed pride, boasts that he has brought to his South Carolina district 90 percent of its lush defense activity — including a Marine Corps air station, an Army depot, a shipyard, a Navy training center, two Polaris missile facilities, a Navy supply center, two Navy hospitals, a Marine Corps recruiting depot, and a payroll that runs $200 million a year.

Only a few members of Congress can benefit so handsomely, naturally, but a considerable majority get some Pentagon money to bolster the economy of their districts. Every now and then a congressman becomes outraged that he is not getting his fair share, and explodes in fine rhetoric. Thus in 1959 Congressman Ken Hechler (Dem.-W.Va.) cried out:

I am firmly against the kind of logrolling which would subject our defense program to narrowly sectional or selfish pulling and hauling.

But I am getting pretty hot under the collar about the way my state of West Virginia is shortchanged in Army, Navy, and Air Force installations. . . . I am going to stand up on my hind legs and roar until West Virginia gets the fair treatment she deserves.[15]

The Pentagon heeded his anguish by increasing his state's allotment of military contracts from $36 million in fiscal 1960 to $162 million in fiscal 1963. All told the military establishment primes the pump with contracts and installations in 363 of the nation's 435 congressional districts, and of course all 50 states.

Who can tell in this game of *quid pro quo* how many legislators vote for a weapons system they don't think is necessary in order to get a contract for their own business community, and how much pork is put into the budget barrel by the Pentagon to lure a congressional vote?

Each dollar, speaking figuratively, makes a friend, and with $45 billion to dispense as procurement each year and a slightly smaller sum for operations, the military has been able to forge a constituency second to none in this land or any land, today or at any time in history. Military spending, says Senator Fulbright, provides "the livelihood of some 10 percent of our work force." Some 22,000 prime contractors and 100,000 subcontractors depend on the Pentagon for some share of their business. It is estimated that the ABM program alone will add cash to the coffers of 15,000 corporations, and derivatively — in jobs — to their employees. The $8 billion spent for research and development each year makes the Pentagon "the largest consumer of research output in the nation." According to the Carnegie Foundation for the Advancement of Teaching the R & D money allocated by Defense, AEC, and NASA to colleges and universities changes "the whole character of many universities' research programs (and in consequence their instructional programs) . . ." Without these sums "faculties in many instances would shrink. Many research efforts would have to be abandoned completely. Others would be sharply curtailed."[16]

Thus, argues Fulbright, "millions of Americans whose only interest is in making a decent living have acquired a vested interest in an economy geared to war. Those benefits, once obtained, are not easily parted with. Every new weapons system or military installation soon acquires a constituency . . ."[17]

Fulbright might have added that it is not only money that gives men a vested interest "in an economy geared to war," but power and prestige as well. In the military itself dollars are certainly secondary to promotion. General Shoup writes:

> The armed forces are not profit-making organizations, and the rewards for excellence in the military profession are acquired in less tangible forms. Thus it is that promotion and the responsibilities of higher command, with the related fringe benefits of quarters, servants, privileges, and prestige, motivates most career officers.[18]

Dollars obviously are a decisive consideration for the large corporations involved in war work, but in other sectors of the military-industrial complex — the labor hierarchy, for instance — the motives are mixed. Many a university dean, for instance, goes along only because he wants a new physics laboratory. Whatever the motives, however, when men gain a vested interest a certain momentum is generated, strong or weak depending on the size of the interest, to defend and extend it. New organizations spring up to create liaison between allies and cement their power; new intellectual weapons are forged to "sell" to the public a point of view favorable to the vested interest. Thus a complex arises which is elitist, fenced off both in terms of special privilege and outlook from the great mass. It feels little obligation to the uninitiate, and either wittingly or unwittingly, seeks to get around popular control.

Consider for instance the way some weapons become realities. In a "posture" statement to the Senate Armed Services Committee early in 1969 Defense Secretary Laird announced he would ask for another $23 million for accelerated design work on a new manned intercontinental bomber called AMSA — advanced manned strategic aircraft. In a budget that runs to $80 billion a year for "defense," $23 million is, to use a phrase made famous by John L. Lewis, "small potatoes." Laird coupled the request, moreover, with the announcement of an economy move: that the Pentagon would cut off its FB-111 program at four squadrons.

On second glance, however, the $23 million was a virtual commitment to spend $12 to $24 *billion* over the next eight years. The small sum would propel the project from what the Pentagon calls the "competitive design phase" — drawings, mock-ups, and wind tunnel testing — to the "contract definition stage." Once at this point it was all but inevitable that a prototype plane would be built at a cost of $1.5 to $2 billion, and after that 240 AMSAs at $50 million each.

Thus, as Senator Proxmire observed, "by an appropriation this year of $23 million, we essentially back into a new manned bomber program which will cost at least $12 billion . . ." and very likely $24 billion, since actual outlay tends to run two or three times the original estimates.[19]

Leaving aside the fact that manned intercontinental bombers may be obsolete in an age of unmanned missiles, and that the U.S. already enjoys a four to one advantage in this field — 646 to 150 for the Soviets — this little incident illustrates the technique by which the military-industrial complex edges forward. No one suggests that this is part of a grand conspiracy. It is simply part of an elan that says the "military knows best" and everyone else ought to defer to it. "Our national security," said Senator Stennis in one of his reports, "can ill afford to have professional judgments of military officials given inadequate weight by their civilian superiors."[20]

Concomitant with the elitist elan, the military-industrial complex vigorously tries to mold the public in its image — for without a near-automatic acceptance by the public of its precepts, everything else would founder. The men of the complex deny this vehemently. The industrialists say they do nothing more than produce weapons. The Pentagon says it only follows civilian orders. The think-tanks say they are only doing research, not making policy. The liaison groups say they are only bringing the Pentagon and industry together to cut red tape. Vice Admiral J. B. Colwell insists in a July-August 1969 issue of *Ordnance*, that the "military-industrial relationship" is simply one of "necessary teamwork."

But consider the evolution and the role of one of the daddies of the military-industrial complex, the American Ordnance Association. Prior to World War I all ordnance was produced in government arsenals; the Great War, however, taxed facilities so much that the military had to turn to private industry for its hardware. Unfortunately neither industry nor the military had any experience in dealing with each other. There was no mechanism by which each could inform itself rapidly what the other was doing or planning; and industry knew very little about how to get around in the bureaucratic maze of government.

To remedy this situation for the future, Bernard Baruch, wartime production czar, helped form the Army Ordnance Association in 1919. Its results during World War II were heartening enough so that AOA's function was extended beyond the Army and its contractors, to *all* the services, and its name changed to *American* Ordnance Association. Today — according to a spokesman, Commander Arthur D. Sullivan (USN retired) — AOA boasts 47,600 members, corporate and individual, paying up to $650 a year dues. Its president is Henry Wallace of U.S. Steel; its executive officer, Major William Ghormley (retired).[21]

As its prospectus points out, AOA is a "liaison between science, industry, and the armed forces in the research, development, and production of superior weapons." Its 22 technical divisions arrange briefings for corporations and engineers that they could not arrange for themselves, and its 41 regional chapters sustain pride in the military establishment by arranging for speakers, by sending delegations to visit defense plants, installations, and naval ships.

On the other hand, when the Pentagon needs help, AOA draws on industry for reciprocal service. For instance, when General Frank Besson was beset by explosions in several Army ammunition plants under his command, AOA sent out a rush call for seven top experts in private business to visit the factories and suggest remedies. "I called Du Pont," says Sullivan, "and asked them for the best man they had, and they gave him to me immediately, free of charge for as long as I needed him." During the Vietnam buildup a couple of years ago, the Army found itself lacking sufficient suppliers for fire control equipment. "Within a week," says Sullivan, "we provided them with a list of 85 qualified companies that had the know-how and equipment to convert to that kind of production."

A half-dozen private military industrial groups function in much the same way and with the same objectives — liaison — as AOA. There is the Association of the U.S. Army, with 104,000 members; the Navy League with 41,000; the Air Force Association with 90,000; the Aerospace Association, a trade group, with 59 corporate members; and the National Security Industrial Association with 425 corporate members paying up to $3,000 a year each in dues. Not all these groups function identically, and they differ somewhat in composition, but their general approach is the same as AOA's: to foster "necessary teamwork."

There is nothing particularly sinister in mechanisms of this sort — if one accepts the assumptions of the Cold War. But "necessary teamwork" ranges far beyond the manufacture of weapons to the manufacture of public opinion.

It could hardly be otherwise, for it would be difficult to win approval for a new weapons system or the military stance generally if the nation was not conditioned to believe that it faces an intractable enemy ready to destroy it. If the danger of being attacked were minimized in the public mind, the military establishment would shrink apace. Cynics call this molding of public opinion the "software" end of the business, as necessary, evidently, as the "hardware" end.

The AOA bimonthly, *Ordnance,* for instance, carries an article in its July-August 1969 issue by Dr. Stefan T. Possony warning that U.S. missile superiority in Europe "is about to disappear." It is folly, says Possony, to think of protecting free Europe "with conventional weapons." What is urgently needed is the deployment of tactical "nuclear armament."

The June 1969 issue of AOA's monthly newsletter is distraught over the "rapid increase in offensive and defensive Soviet missile capability," which it says puts the lie to Russian pretensions at "limitation of the arms race." After pointing to Cuban attempts to foment revolution in Latin America, the Soviet invasion of Czechoslovakia in August 1968, the North

Vietnamese attempt to "force their will on South Vietnam with communist arms," the Soviet fleet in the Mediterranean — the publication casts its darts at the "neophyte legislators, unrealistic scientists, and many unthinking dupes, who would weaken the defense of the United States." A month later, when the ABM issue was before the public, the same newsletter commented that "the amount of opposition to the ABM is alarming. The hard evidence shows that too many fail to understand the ruthlessly aggressive ambitions of communist leaders."

Such propaganda obviously goes beyond the "necessary teamwork" for making weapons. It is a political function with a political purpose. Even more, it is part of an orchestrated effort by all segments of the military-industrial complex to guide public opinion in a single direction — and there, as the bard said, lies the rub.

The militarist theorems themselves usually originate in think-tanks and private research organizations as erudite documents. The ideas are then transformed into more popular versions and transmitted to the public in many different ways. By way of example, when ABM became a great issue in 1969 the American Security Council "underwrote a study by 31 leading experts from the Council's Subcommittee on National Strategy to investigate the problem." The subcommittee was headed by Dr. Willard F. Libby, director of the Institute of Geophysics and Planetary Physics; Dr. William J. Thaler, chairman of the physics department at Georgetown University; and General Nathan F. Twining (retired), former chairman of the Joint Chiefs of Staff. Its findings were published in a 72-page study: "USSR vs USA" (The ABM and the Changed Strategic Military Balance). Around the same time the Foreign Policy Research Institute of the University of Pennsylvania, strongly oriented toward the Pentagon and a recipient of many of its research contracts, rushed into print with a volume: *Safeguard: Why the ABM Makes Sense.* Along with 15 articles *for* the ABM it carried a single piece by Dr. Jerome Wiesner against it, in order, as the publishers say, "to make the volume as complete as possible." The Hudson Institute, headed by Herman Kahn, also prepared a book on the subject — while it held a $70,253 contract for a secret study of the strategic implications of ABM. Kahn denied there was any "conflict of interest," but Senator Edward M. Kennedy (Dem.-Mass.) insisted that the work "appears to be financed in part by the Department of Defense."[22]

Simultaneously the Pentagon itself elaborated a comprehensive plan to "sell" ABM. Appropriately, it was marked "classified" — for "national security" reasons. Drafted by Lieutenant General Alfred E. Starbird and approved by Army Secretary Stanley R. Resor, it outlined a variety of activities — feeding information to technical publications to write favorable articles; conducting orientation tours for the press, Congressmen, military personnel, scientific, fraternal, and civil groups; and generally providing, as *Congressional Quarterly* called it, a "favorable public attitude" toward the placing of sites near major cities.[23] Reporters were offered a trip by Resor to Kwajalein and New Mexico to see test firings of ABM missiles at firsthand. Building trades labor leaders were given a special briefing on the subject, in return for which at least two large unions — the carpenters' and the electrical workers' — carried pro-ABM pieces in their magazines.[24]

The secret plan was brought to light by a Washington newspaper and had to be canceled because of the resulting public outcry, in and out of Congress. The nation seemed to be less tolerant of the Pentagon using taxpayers' money to engage in political propaganda than it had been during the UMT campaigns. But private groups took up where the Pentagon left off.

One such "spontaneous grassroots" organization was the Citizens' Committee for Peace and Security, which published newspaper advertisements throughout the country claiming that "84 percent of all Americans say that the United States should have an ABM system." This was surprising in view of the Gallup poll which showed 25 percent in favor, 15 percent opposed, and a majority with no opinion. Equally surprising was the assertion in the ad that "the Russians have already deployed their own ABM system," a claim which William J. Casey, a New York lawyer who headed the committee admitted was "a little fuzzy" and which Senator Fulbright said was plain "untrue."

Subsequently the Senate Foreign Relations Committee revealed that among the signers of the ad were 11 key officials of eight companies which held more than $150 million in ABM contracts, including five of the 12 largest — IBM, Motorola, Sperry-Rand, General Electric, and Martin-Marietta — as well as Lockheed, Brunswick, and American Machine & Foundry.[25] It is safe to assume that at least some of these companies were charging off their contributions for the Citizens' Committee as deductible expenses on their defense contracts. It was also learned that Colonel Charles West, the committee's chief staffman, was doing work in mobilizing support for the program not from any private office but from an office in the White House where he was serving as a "consultant" to Presidential aide Colonel Bruce Jacobs. Jacobs, it turned out, was an advisor to the right-wing National Security Information Center, from which West was on leave of absence, and for which Casey served as a director. Parenthetically, Casey was nominated by President Nixon to be an advisor, of all places, to the Arms Control and Disarmament Agency.

Contrary to the image it cultivates of not participating in civilian affairs, the Pentagon, both through its allies and itself, is heavily involved in shaping public opinion. If it agrees with the content of a movie, for instance, it will help a producer film it — and on very generous terms. One such movie done recently was *The Green Berets*, which promoted a favorable view both of the military and of the war in Vietnam. Congressman Benjamin S. Rosenthal (Dem.-N.Y.) charged in June 1969 that the Army had billed John Wayne and his Batjac Company $18,623.64 for 107 days of using its facilities in Fort Benning, Georgia, to produce the movie. The actual cost to the Army for utilities in three buildings, 85 hours of flying time for an undesignated number of UH-1 helicopters, for M-16 rifles, bulldozers, trucks, and the Pentagon-assigned project officer who worked with it, said Rosenthal, probably was a million dollars or more.[26] The Army said it had been "properly reimbursed," and perhaps it had. *Green Berets* was an excellent advertisement. The military also produces its own films, scores of them, such as *The Army and Vietnam, Strategy for Peace* (about the Strategic

Air Command), and the like. It solicits and receives a considerable amount of free time on television and radio, and it places many articles with friendly media. The director of its Office of Public Information exulted one year that the *Saturday Evening Post*, as an indication of its collaboration with DOD, had carried 57 articles the year before favorable to the Pentagon.[27] A military spokesman in 1969 could not say how many people were employed in public information because some serve in dual capacities. But back in 1951 Senator Harry F. Byrd reported that DOD "this year is using 3,022 civilians and uniformed persons in advertising, publicity, and public relations jobs at a payroll cost of $10,109,109."[28]

What the Pentagon fails to do to "sell" itself is done by other segments of the military-industrial complex, much of it — directly or indirectly — with government funds.

The devilry that is created by this purposive effort at opinion molding is illustrated by the three "missile gap" scares of the past nine years. The first one in 1960 was promoted by DOD and its allies, says former Budget Director Charles L. Schultze, "at a time when there was not a single Soviet ICBM (intercontinental ballistic missile) deployed." The nation "was led to near hysteria over the prospect that the Russians might have large numbers of missiles within a very few years. Later we learned that they actually built only three percent of the missiles predicted by 1963. . ."

The second gap was an "anti-missile gap," the carefully cultivated impression that the Soviets were forging an ABM system throughout their country. This resulted in a demand to target more warheads on the Soviet Union and to develop the MIRV so that the total of targetable warheads might increase from 2,400 to 8,000 or 10,000. Later it was found that the Russians had only a small ABM system around Moscow, which is now obsolete.

In 1969 a third missile gap was manufactured, involving the Russian SS-9 which is described as a "first strike weapon against our Minuteman force." To respond to this challenge, we are told, the nation now requires the Safeguard ABM — this despite the fact that our 41 invulnerable Polaris submarines alone can each destroy 12 Soviet urban centers, "not to mention the destruction which could be inflicted by our fleet of B-52 bombers and the tactical aircraft we have deployed around the world."[29]

What begins as an article in one of the military-industrial journals or as a document in a public or private think-tank becomes eventually what John Kenneth Galbraith calls a "conventional wisdom." It is repeated by top Pentagon and government offcials, who command headlines, and by friendly columnists and newspaper editors, until a vast majority of the nation begins to believe it. Thus there arises such firm "wisdom" as:

"If we don't fight them in Vietnam we'll have to fight them in California."

"You can't trust the Russians to live up to any treaty," or, as Representative Rivers puts it, "I have no confidence in any Communist anywhere on earth."

"We have to fight fire with fire" — guns with guns.

Obviously any private person or group has a right to its opinion. But there is a *public* quality to this opinion-shaping campaign by the military-industrial complex — first, because much of it is paid for directly or indirectly by the government, and second, because it is a self-serving effort to gain dollars or power from public institutions.

Douglas Aircraft, for instance, was paid $89,500 by the Army to do a study called "Pax Americana," outlining world political patterns through 1985. Not surprisingly, it concluded that "the United States is not an imperialistic nation," but it has "acquired imperial responsibilities."[30] "Imperial responsibilities" is a proper formula for maintaining contingency forces, bases around the world, and a substantial enough military arm for any emergency. And while the report was classified, it is available to insiders and through them will become the rationale used by many military-industrial complex publications and speakers to justify the arms race. General Electric, Westinghouse, and many other large firms, as well as AOA, play the same game of prognostication, almost always ending with the conclusion that America must maintain and enlarge its military establishment because there is little hope of peace.

The image of the future in these surveys somehow tends to confirm industry wishes. Thus a report by the Electronics Industries Association in 1967, on what can be expected after Vietnam, concluded that arms control agreements "during the next decade are unlikely," and the "likelihood of limited war will increase." Bernard D. Nossiter, a reporter for the *Washington Post*, was shown the private "blue books" of a number of large corporations in Texas, each one projecting a sharp rise in military sales. LTV Aerospace Corporation estimates its orders will jump from $530 million in 1968 to $1.3 billion by 1973. There's no need to worry about social programs draining off money from defense spending, Samuel F. Downer, an LTV vice-president, told Nossiter, because if "you're the President . . . you can't sell Harlem and Watts but you can sell self-preservation. . . . We're going to increase defense budgets as long as those bastards in Russia are ahead of us. The American people understand this."[31]

This is not the voice of the lunatic fringe, but of solid respectable businessmen, and in a dozen different ways that voice filters down to the public.

Among the most active transmission belts for hard-line indoctrination is the American Security Council and its spin-off, the Institute for American Strategy, both headed by an ex-FBI agent, John M. Fisher, and sired by Brigadier General Robert E. Wood, late board chairman of Sears, Roebuck. Apart from a galaxy of big business representatives and retired military officers, the twin organizations included on their boards at various times eminent figures in the academic community, as well as the former Chicago superintendent of schools, Benjamin C. Willis, and the present Illinois superintendent of public instruction, Ray Page. The American Security Council, as originally conceived, was a blacklisting organization, supplying information on employees to member companies from its one-million card-file of "subversives." Its scope now is much wider.

Both groups join together for a host of seminars and educational projects, such as TV courses for high school teachers on the nature of communism, or a school for gubernatorial aides at the 1964 National Governors' Conference. Among the materials they distribute is a cartoon edition of General Thomas S. Power's book *Design for Survival*, which calls for the use of tactical nuclear weapons, denounces disarmament, and makes the claim that the U.S. has been "too trusting, altruistic, generous, too forgiving — to the point that international gangsters are encouraged to pillage, burn, kill, and dictate." A radio program, which usually features former Representative Walter Judd and used to include Senator Thomas Dodd, is heard over 1,000 stations every day.

Their most ambitious effort is the Freedom Studies Center, a "West Point" of psychological-political warfare frankly aimed at training Cold War leadership. Invited to participate are key staff members of Congress, government employees, church leaders, journalists, labor officials, and executives of voluntary organizations. Army Chief of Staff William C. Westmoreland was the distinguished guest lecturer at a series of its seminars in February 1969. Other lecturers included the peripatetic Stefan Possony and Frank J. Johnson. Johnson's program for "peace" calls for an American invasion of Albania and Cuba, followed by "paramilitary warfare" elsewhere in the communist world, as well as unleashing Chiang Kai-shek to attack mainland China, and South Vietnam to invade North Vietnam.[32]

More sophisticated — and perhaps more important — are a number of private research groups, usually but not always associated with universities, such as the Hoover Institution at Stanford, the Center for Strategic and International Studies at Georgetown, the Foreign Policy Research Institute at the University of Pennsylvania, and William J. Baroody's American Enterprise Institute for Public Policy Research. They publish scholarly tracts, such as those by Baroody's AEI, on arms control, "The Soviet Military Technological Challenge," the "Economic Impact of the Vietnam War," "Sino-Soviet Rivalry." Their seminars, which sometimes invite liberals like Arthur Schlesinger, Jr., include a Who's Who of the pro-military brain trust — Presidential aide Henry A. Kissinger; G. Warren Nutter, now a major official in the Pentagon; Edward Teller; W. Glenn Campbell of the Hoover Institution; Alvin J. Cottrell, who served for three years on the faculty of the National War College.

Surveying the roster of these institutions one gets an idea of the interlocking and far-flung character of the military-industrial complex. Admiral Arleigh Burke (retired), chairman of the Georgetown Center, is a past president of AOA, a director of Chrysler, Texaco, Newport News Shipbuilding, Thiokol Chemical — and was a vice-chairman of President Nixon's task force on national security. His philosophy is summed up in the pithy statement that "between the free West and the communist movement there can be no reconciliation, no real coexistence. The confrontation is absolute." Colonel William Kintner, editor of the pro-ABM book referred to above, is deputy director of the Institute at Pennsylvania and was once a planning officer with the Army Chief of Staff. Dr. Robert Strausz-Hupe, director of the Institute, was a member of Nixon's foreign policy task force, and before that an advisor to Presidential-aspirant Goldwater in 1964. Baroody of AEI was also a Goldwater brain truster in 1964, and his son is on the staff of Defense Secretary Laird.

Another picturesque figure is W. Glenn Campbell, director of the Hoover Institution at Stanford. A former professor at Harvard, for five years an employee of the U.S. Chamber of Commerce for whom he wrote reports critical of social security and compulsory health insurance, and later research director for Baroody's AEI, Campbell believes the purpose of his institution is "to demonstrate the evils of Karl Marx — whether communism, socialism, economic materialism, or atheism — thus to protect the American way of life from such ideologies, their conspiracies, and to reaffirm the validities of the American system." His "conservative views on education," writes Berkeley Rice in a well-researched article for *The Washington Monthly*, "so impressed California's Governor Ronald Reagan that the governor appointed him to the Board of Regents . . ."[33] On Campbell's board of advisors at the institution have been key executives from the major corporations — Standard of New Jersey, Mobil, U.S. Steel, Republic Steel, Lockheed. "Of the 56 current advisory board members," Rice reports, "only two are educators." An active member of this board and co-chairman of the fund drive was David Packard, now Deputy Secretary of Defense. Another alumnus is Richard V. Allen, a senior staff member of the National Security Council.

Men like Campbell and officers of other research organizations and think-tanks seldom come into the limelight. But their views are heard on the public podium from the lips of high government officials and military leaders they advise, and in thousands of articles in the pro-military and general press. And they fan out from there so that if the effect is subtle, it is nonetheless massive.

In a speech to the National War College in May 1969, Senator Fulbright spoke of "changes which are slowly undermining democratic procedure and values, and which . . . have set us on the path toward authoritarian government." One of the most significant steps toward forging a political monopoly by the military-industrial complex, is the synthetic manufacture of public opinion. Dr. Ralph McDonald of the National Education Association said many years ago that there are two ways of destroying freedom — through concentration camps and through "influencing public opinion."[34] No Americans are in concentration camps today, but given the ceaseless bombardment of the public with propaganda that originates from, and is partly paid by, the Pentagon, as well as the allies who depend on it, there is grave doubt about the free character of public opinion.

CHAPTER FOUR

The Military Syndrome

In the Middle Ages wars were fought by the military class exclusively; the general population was virtually uninvolved. As technology has advanced, however, more and more layers of the civilian force have become integral parts of the military operation. Millions of workers and thousands of corporations today produce the ordnance that the military itself used to produce. Scientists and academics research and engineer a qualitatively new generation of weapons, and carry on a variety of psychological and social tasks such as propaganda and pacification. In addition, millions of people are inducted for civil defense. The civilian has become a target for destruction by the enemy just like the soldier. Every worker that is killed and every factory that is immobilized reduces the supply of weaponry, food, and materiel to the soldier on the battlefield. To be effective, then, the military must guarantee its "rear" as much as its "front," and civilians who dig out from under a bombing raid, provide medical attention, and rebuild shattered industries, are as essential to the total effort as bombardiers who drop bombs.

The phenomenon of war today requires a total coordination between civilians in uniform and civilians in overalls — or between "soldiers" in overalls and soldiers in uniform — and all kinds of mechanisms and laws are forged for that purpose. During World War II, for instance, agencies were created to control

wages, prices, manpower, material-allotment, collective bargaining — so that the economy behind the lines would not collapse.
The Smith Act and the House Committee on Un-American
Activities were designed — though clumsily — to "protect" the
population from antiwar elements who might sow defeatism.
To fight a war a nation needs not only discipline at the front but
"national unity," discipline, behind the lines. It is only natural,
therefore, that the military should have an interest in what takes
place on the domestic scene and should try to influence it. It
must look to the rear not only for its war materiel, but it has a
definite stake in civilian morale. If a defeatist sentiment should
develop, as it did in the Vietnam War, it can have a serious impact
on the way the war is fought, or whether it can be fought at all.

Inevitably, then, whether in peacetime or in wartime, a military
syndrome results from the military function. Whether the purpose of our postwar military establishment is "defense," as the
militarists say, or "global expansion," as seems evident from the
record, there is a pitiless logic to militarism. Those with a stake
in preparedness weld themselves into a military-complex that
ranges far beyond the military itself, just as the military function
now ranges far beyond the soldier on the line. Preparedness as
a matter of course must concern itself with national unity, and
national unity requires the manufacture of public opinion —
first, to assure a popular stance that pressures the Executive and
Congress to accept the military's estimate of its requirements;
and second, to create the kind of discipline within the population
that will be needed when and if hostilities break out.

It is this military syndrome which accounts for two important
impulses in the present American way of life: (1) the trend to
exclude the public from decision-making, and, as a consequence,
governmental secrecy, deception, and measures to impose "loyalty"; (2) the trend of the military to acquire more and more
civilian functions.

"Information," said former Assistant Defense Secretary
Arthur Sylvester some years ago, "is power. In the beginning
was the word. It is more powerful than the bomb and the gun."[1]
If this is true it raises some fundamental questions about "govern-

ment by consent of the governed." If the governed are denied the facts on which to make an intelligent assessment of government plans and activity — or are given false facts — their right to consent is effectively abrogated. Unfortunately, however, this is exactly what has been happening, and it is summarized in the increasing complaints by legislators about secrecy and by publicists about the credibility gap.

It is ironic that at a time when the Defense Department and the Executive generally release far more material to the media than ever in the past, they are also withholding much more, and precisely that information which is of the highest priority as far as the public is concerned. A reporter who visits the Pentagon's public information office can get the name of an air base in Thailand or Brazil within minutes. The reception is courteous and businesslike. But there are times when prying the facts out of DOD is like trying to break into Fort Knox with a screwdriver.

In its May 1969 report, Senator Proxmire's Subcommittee on Economy in Government carries a highly unusual seven-page indictment of DOD for "excessive secrecy and employee control" — specifically that the Pentagon refused information, hid information, and threatened to discipline an employee for testifying freely.[2]

One of the witnesses before the subcommittee was John M. Malloy, Deputy Assistant Secretary of Defense for procurement, who was accompanied by three aides, all with substantial titles. These were men responsible for buying weapons, pricing them, and auditing the contracts. Yet they "didn't know" whether the costs of the multibillion C-5A cargo plane contract with Lockheed had exceeded original estimates. Nor could they make a judgment on what the company's profits would be as a percentage of investment.

The subcommittee was particularly disturbed about the treatment accorded the Government Accounting Office (GAO), which it had asked to look into the matter. GAO has been called the "conscience of the government," and under the Budget and Accounting Act is specifically given access to the records of government agencies. But in this instance Air Force Secretary Robert

H. Charles refused to give it cost information on the C-5A —
"in order to avoid possible compromise of negotiations" for a
second batch of planes. No national security issue was involved,
but if the costs were made known it might somehow affect future
contract negotiations — exactly how is not made clear. The data
was later offered GAO, according to the testimony of Frank H.
Weitzel, Assistant Comptroller General of the United States,
only if it would agree not to make it public. Finally, after cooling
its heels for seven weeks GAO was given a short letter, just two
days before its representatives were to testify — and "with less
than complete" information.

Had it not been for an efficiency expert in the Air Force, A.
Ernest Fitzgerald, who testified against the wishes of his superiors, the strange story of how Lockheed exceeded original cost
estimates by $2 billion might still be buried. The Air Force,
according to Proxmire's Subcommittee, first ordered Fitzgerald
not to appear as a witness, then assigned him to be merely a
"back-up" witness, and relented finally only under considerable
congressional pressure. Proxmire also claims that Fitzgerald was
instructed not to provide a written supplemental statement, and
that when such a document was transmitted, after two months,
it turned out to have been written by someone else, and contained information that differed from Fitzgerald's. For his zeal
Fitzgerald was reassigned by the Pentagon to checking cost
overruns on a 20-lane bowling alley owned by the military in
Thailand and at Air Force mess halls.[3] Later he was fired.

Subcommittee requests for overrun data on the SRAM (short-
range attack missile) were denied because this, too, would preju-
dice "negotiations with the contractor" — another contractor.
And information about overruns in the B-52, Minuteman, F-4,
and F-11 programs were similarly refused: this time because
they "would permit [the contractors] a meaningful comparison
with the experience on the C-5." On these theories it would seem
that Congress is entitled to no information on weapons' costs at
any time.

The mania for secrecy is a relatively new phenomenon in the
United States. Under the Atomic Energy Act of 1946 govern-

ment agencies were authorized to withhold news from the public about fission and atomic energy on the theory this would be gratuitous intelligence for the Soviets. President Eisenhower's Order 10501 of November 1953 extended the right to classify information, in varying degrees, to 24 other agencies.

These measures, however, were aimed at denying national security data to a potential enemy, not at denying nonsensitive information to the American people. Yet today there are thousands of documents held from public view by Pentagon labels of "classified," "confidential," "secret," or "top secret," many of which have no relevance whatsoever to security. And, as in the Proxmire subcommittee case, information is simply refused when it does not suit the Pentagon's purposes.

The Army, on March 4, 1969, admitted to a closed session of a congressional committee — according to *Congressional Quarterly* — that the cost of chemical and biological weapons had "been hidden and scattered throughout the defense budget for years."[4] Why should such facts be disguised, any more than other cost figures of the defense budget? *Science* magazine (January 1967) is probably correct when it says that the military wants such information secret because it is "easily misunderstood and because it provokes the most emotional distress and moral turbulence."

Whether the cost of weapons and CBW should or should not be hidden, there would seem to be little reason for classifying research in the social science field. Yet during 1967 alone, according to John S. Foster, Jr., director of defense, research, and engineering, 76 social science studies paid for by DOD were marked "classified."[5] The Douglas Aircraft document on "Projected World Patterns — 1985" was labeled secret even before the contract to write it was signed — on the grounds of "possible foreign policy sensitivity." Perhaps most ludicrous of all was the attachment of a "secret" label to *newspaper clippings* about a Navy communications project in Wisconsin. Clearly someone had gone too far, for on February 12, 1969, the *Washington Star* reported that DOD had finally removed the secrecy tag.

A few years ago the Institute for Defense Analysis, the

Pentagon-subsidized think-tank, prepared a study of the Tonkin Gulf incidents of 1964. Those incidents, in which North Vietnamese boats allegedly had fired torpedoes at American destroyers, were the basis, it will be recalled, of the Tonkin Gulf resolution by Congress which the Johnson administration later claimed was a "functional equivalent" of a declaration of war.

Since the escalation of hostilities in Vietnam, Senator Fulbright and others have had second thoughts about having voted for the resolution — first because President Johnson had stretched a mandate to "retaliate" into a mandate for full-scale bombing and sending troops to Vietnam, but, equally important, because information uncovered by newsmen in the meantime indicated that the destroyers may have been a cover for a *South* Vietnamese attack on two North Vietnamese islands, and the U.S. ships may very well have been in Hanoi's waters. Be that as it may, the chairman of the Committee on Foreign Relations was entitled to any scrap of information available on the subject, since under the Constitution (Article 1, Section 8) only Congress has the right to declare war, and under the well-known principle of "checks and balances" Congress has the inalienable authority to check up on the President. If there was anything in the IDA study that showed the Chief Executive had made a misjudgment or had distorted the facts, Fulbright, of all people, had the right to know.

But from Secretary McNamara on down, DOD has refused to give Fulbright access to the document, on the peculiar ground that "the author of the study did not have access to certain sources of information."[6] When the senator asked Dr. Foster, "What value is this study . . . under such circumstances?" he was coldly informed that "the value was availability of the document to the officials of the Department of Defense." It was available, in other words, to the generals and their civilian cohorts, but not to Fulbright — and through him to the public. The excuse used was so flimsy that even Senator Karl Mundt, a man of heavily hawkish sentiments, could not restrain his sarcasm: "Do you have a fictional section in this outfit [DOD]," he demanded, "where they say 'Write me a fictional story or a Buck Rogers story about it, or do you have someone who rides herd to see that the man who makes the study is competent to make it?"

Equally frustrating is the proclivity of DOD to withhold details of secret military agreements which, under some circumstances, can plunge the nation into actual war. No one outside the cloistered inner circle knows how many such understandings there are or exactly what they encompass. *U.S. News & World Report* (July 21, 1969) claims there are "at least 24" with nations such as Spain, Iran, Jordan, Congo Republic (Léopoldville), Ethiopia, Tunisia, etc. How much the United States is committed in each case is not clear. The Congo Republic embassy in Washington, for instance, insists it has no military agreement with the United States. But a spokesman concedes that there have been ad hoc arrangements in 1964 and 1967 in which the American ambassador at Léopoldville agreed to "logistical support" to put down "mercenaries." The logistical support, if *The New York Times* accounts are true, involved bombers and transport planes, as well as "diplomats" who guided the planes to their destinations.[7]

Whatever the "commitment" with the Congo, however, there is little question that some of these pacts are wide-ranging. In 1962 Secretary of State Dean Rusk signed an agreement with the foreign minister of Thailand, Thanat Khoman, pledging that the United States would defend the ancient nation of Siam not only from outside aggression but from civil war.[8] "Under the secret agreement," writes Flora Lewis, "the United States has been providing Thailand with something between $175 million and $250 million a year for Thai forces. The aid has been hidden in the defense budget under other programs so that Congress never knew what the money was going for."[9]

After the Vietnam War heated up in 1965 Washington built sizable air bases in Thailand and eventually dispatched 48,000 soldiers to the country, some acting as "advisors" similar in status to the original 22,000 troops dispatched to Vietnam by President Kennedy. It was at this point that Lieutenant General Richard G. Stillwell, an old CIA hand then in charge of the troops, signed a secret military agreement with the Thai called a "contingency agreement." It is detailed enough, in the opinion of senators who have seen it, to spell out the number of American soldiers to be sent in, and the theaters of operation they were to be responsible for in case of combat. Fulbright says the plan is known as COMUSTAF Plan 1-64.[10]

Yet Fulbright's foreign affairs committee — which stumbled on the existence of this document only in the course of investigating a similar one for Spain — has been refused a copy of the agreement. "In this case — as in the case of any contingency plan," Acting Secretary of State Elliot L. Richardson wrote Fulbright, "the Department of Defense is extremely reluctant to allow the full text to get out of its own hands," but DOD was willing to give the senator "an extensive briefing on these plans by officers from the Joint Chiefs of Staff."[11] State insisted it was merely a *contingency* plan. But back in 1967 Graham Martin, U.S. ambassador to Thailand, told writer Louis Lomax that "our commitment to Thailand is total and irrevocable." Lomax asked: "Does that mean our men will die, if necessary, to defend the current government in Bangkok?" The reply was an unequivocal "Yes."[12] What it amounts to, if the ambassador's version is correct, is that a secret military pact — never discussed, approved, or even seen by Congress — has committed the United States to a Vietnamese-type war.

The partial scuttling of the Senate's treaty power is simply another feature of the military syndrome. Under the Constitution, treaties require a two-thirds vote of the upper chamber to be ratified. On many occasions the Senate has withheld its sanction, the best known example being the Treaty of Versailles. Executive agreements, by contrast, are entered into on matters of minor consequence that do not, presumably, alter national policy. In 1939, according to figures published by Hans Morgenthau, "10 treaties were concluded by the United States as over against 26 executive agreements. The corresponding figures for the following years are eloquent: 1940: 12-20, 1941: 15-39 . . . 1963: 9-248, 1964: 13-231, 1965: 5-197, 1966: 10-242, 1967: 10-218, 1968: 57-226."[13] More and more what used to be the subject of a treaty requiring Senate confirmation, has become the subject of an executive pact, often buried under a top secret classification.

A war machine demands discipline, obedience, conformity, and subordination to it of all facets of national life. You cannot win a war without national unity, without "everyone pulling together." Inevitably, then, that *elan* seeps into the whole culture. The military and the Executive withhold information from the public, first to keep it from the enemy, then in order not to tarnish their own image (as in cost overruns), and finally not to injure public sensibilities, which also disturbs national unity (as in the case of chemical and biological weapons, and Thailand).

"I shall withhold from neither the Congress nor the people," said President Kennedy in his State of the Union message, January 30, 1961, "any fact or report, past, present, or future, which is necessary for an informed judgment of our conduct or hazards." This doctrine has been affirmed on ceremonial occasions by all other Presidents, before and after. But the reality has not been consonant with the rhetoric; a militarist approach to policy demands militaristic secrecy.

The fact that the Pentagon had a MIRV program, for instance, was kept secret from most members of Congress for three years.[14] MIRV — the multi-weapon missile that can be targeted independently — is not just another weapon. It changes the whole character of the arms race, because with the same number of missiles it is possible to mount three or four times as many hydrogen bombs — at least — as before. If either the United States or the Soviet Union begins deploying them, anxieties on both sides will mount by geometric progression — because there is no way of knowing either through direct observation or through spy satellites how many weapons are on a missile when it is in its silo. And with the great increase in targeted warheads — from 2,400 to 8,000 or 10,000 — each side will more easily assume that the other is getting ready to strike first. The mischief that can ensue is frightening to contemplate; so that, if there is anything that bears on basic national policy, it is the MIRV. Yet, except for the handful of men in the Armed Services Committee, Congress itself was not informed of this development, and the public scratched out the facts after three long years only as a result of judicious leaks to the press.

Repeatedly, Americans wake up to find themselves on the brink of war without having known in advance the facts behind it, and without having had a chance either themselves or through their representatives to discuss policy. That has been true of Vietnam, the Dominican crisis, the Lebanese landing, the Congo, and very likely of the October 1962 missile crisis. The American people get plenty of information about many matters — though all too often on trivia, such as a Presidential visit to Main Street in San Clemente, California — but on momentous issues they are more often than not left in the cold.

On January 17, 1966 a U.S. B-52 collided with a KC-135 refueling plane and exploded over the village of Palomares, Spain — losing four 25-megaton H-bombs it was carrying. Under some circumstances this might have become a major international crisis — if the bombs had been dropped near the Czech border, for instance, or in Berlin. The American people were certainly entitled to know what kind of risks their government was taking in their name.

But for days thereafter Colonel Barnett "Skippy" Young, an Air Force information officer, insisted that the hundreds of men, planes, ships, and special equipment brought into the area on the double were searching only for "parts of the planes." Even as Spanish civil guards were being taken to hospitals with radio-activity burns, Young answered questions about the plane's cargo with a tight-lipped "no comment." Two newsmen finally coaxed the story out of a garrulous sergeant who told them that three of the four bombs had been recovered but "there's still one bomb missing." Colonel Young, however, continued to be mysteriously ambiguous.

Here is an excerpt from one of his press conferences:

Q. How many ships are offshore today, Colonel?
A. Ships? All I can say is that certain elements of the U.S. Navy are here.
Q. Has the missing bomb been found yet?
A. I know absolutely nothing about a lost bomb.

Q. When will the recovering submarines arrive, Colonel?

A. No comment. Do you really think you're going to see them? They won't make low passes over Palomares you know. They don't fly.

Q. Is there any risk of radiation, or are you merely taking precautions?

A. No comment.

Q. Where can we get information, Colonel?

A. From me. I have no comment to make about anything, and I cannot comment on why I have to say no comment.[15]

Here, as in so many instances, the information was being withheld not because it gave the Soviets gratuitous intelligence but because it is part of the syndrome to be secretive, especially when an incident puts officials in a bad light. The Russians had an intelligence "trawler" in the waters nearby and unquestionably could piece together what was happening. Every military reporter in the world knew that the Strategic Air Command was patrolling Europe with large numbers of aircraft armed with nuclear weapons. The Spanish government was aware of what had happened: its civil guards were patrolling the Palomares area to prevent villagers from venturing into their fields where they might be subject to radiation hazards. The withholding of information was aimed only at the American people for fear they might learn that this was only one of at least 13 similar accidents with nuclear weapons that had taken place in the previous eight years.[16] Had they had the information, the American people might have questioned the policy of nuclear flights.

Woodrow Wilson told a Kansas City audience in 1919:

You know, my fellow citizens, what armaments mean: great standing armies, great stores of war materials. . . . So soon as you have a military class, it does not make any difference what your form of government is: if you are determined to be armed to the teeth, you must obey the orders and directions of the only men who can control the great machinery of war. Elections are of minor importance.[17]

In the military syndrome, the citizenry is removed as far as possible from the decision-making process. "The military," writes General Shoup, "is indoctrinated to be secretive, devious, and misleading in its plans and operations."[18] These are traits that are obviously necessary for waging war. In a militarily-oriented society, unfortunately, the Government itself begins to take on these characteristics. In many critical situations it refuses information or gives misleading information — or both. At the very time when the public needs data most — to either endorse what its government is doing or to pressure it to change — it is denied it or deliberately given false data.

When the U-2 piloted by Gary Powers disappeared while on a spy mission over Soviet territory in 1960, the Eisenhower administration said at first that the plane had been lost while "gathering weather information." This "small" incident may have had an important impact on history, for it torpedoed a scheduled summit meeting between Eisenhower and Soviet leader Nikita Khrushchev which might have improved the relations between their countries. Yet the American people were never told in advance that their government was violating a bushel load of international treaties by repeatedly flying over the air space of the Soviet Union, and when the fact was accidentally disclosed the Government tried to cover up with a falsehood.

When the Johnson administration began building air bases in Thailand it claimed it was for the Siamese Navy (which at that time was said to have one plane). In fact, as everyone is aware today, it was for American bombers to use in bombing North Vietnam. On April 28, 1965 President Johnson, appearing unscheduled on television, said he was sending Marines to the Dominican Republic "in order to give protection to hundreds of Americans . . . and to escort them safely back to this country." The President failed to report that discussions had been held in his administration on military measures to prevent "a communist takeover," or that he had so informed leaders of Congress just before the speech. Within a day it was clear that the Marines in fact were there to help suppress a revolution against an American-supported junta.[19]

During the 1960 election campaign Vice President Nixon denounced John F. Kennedy for suggesting that the United States give aid to Cuban exiles to fight Castro. This irresponsible suggestion, Nixon said, violates "five treaties with Latin America . . . in which we've agreed not to intervene in the internal affairs of any other country." Kennedy's suggestion, he said, was "the most shockingly reckless proposal ever made in our history by a Presidential candidate during a campaign."[20] If we were to follow the course outlined by Kennedy "we would lose all of our friends in Latin America, we would probably be condemned in the United Nations, and we would probably not accomplish our objective."

No statement could be more definitive. But as is now well known, Nixon himself had suggested this plan and knew that the United States was already training Cuban exiles, paying their wages, supplying them with arms, and arranging for Guatemala to set up a secret base for them. While Fidel Castro was in the United States in April 1959 Nixon had had a three-hour talk with him, after which he drafted a three-page memorandum urging President Eisenhower to start preparing the Cuban refugees for an assault on the Caribbean island. Subsequently, in his book, *Six Crises*, Nixon revealed that he had attacked a plan to which he was committed "privately," because he believed JFK's statement endangered American "security."

The Bay of Pigs incident made prevaricators out of many people in high office. On April 19, 1960, in a letter to the Student Federation of Chile, Eisenhower insisted that "no official of this administration has ever made any public statements or committed any acts which may be reasonably construed as unfriendly toward the Cuban government and people." Just a month and two days before, as Eisenhower admitted more than a year later when he was out of office, the President had given the CIA instructions "to help these people [the exiles] organize and to help train them and equip them." It is hard to visualize an act more unfriendly than training counter-revolutionaries to overthrow a government.

When the exile contingent had been defeated, historian Arthur Schlesinger, Jr., a Kennedy aide, gave out the deliberately false story to *The New York Times* — to save face — that Operation Pluto was only a minor foray, involving only 200 to 300 men (it actually involved 1,400).[21] Schlesinger, who had opposed the Bay of Pigs venture, stated four years later: "I do not regard my having told this to *The New York Times* as my finest hour in government. Conceivably it might have been better for me to resign and refuse to give out the cover story."

Kennedy himself evidently had some second thoughts about the secrecy and deception practiced in the Cuban operation. "If you had printed more about the invasion," he told Turner Catledge, executive editor of *The New York Times*, "you would have saved us from a colossal mistake." *The Times* had decided in the "national interest" not to publish what it knew about invasion plans. What Kennedy was implying was that had it done so the pressure of an informed public might have saved his administration from its folly.

Unfortunately the public is seldom given this opportunity; it is spoon-fed "facts" which are designed to placate it, rather than inform. "Once again," reads a dispatch in the *Chicago Daily News* (February 7, 1967), "the Pentagon has been caught in a credibility gap in connection with Vietnam. It has now acknowledged that U.S. aircraft losses there are three times as high as the officially announced figure." Previously DOD had confined its disclosures to the 622 combat planes lost from January 1, 1961 to January 31, 1967, but it now conceded that "planes lost in accidents, lost on the ground from enemy sabotage and mortar fire, or planes that ran out of fuel and had to ditch at sea" brought the figure up to 1,172 — plus another 600 helicopters lost.

The record of misinformation can be multiplied endlessly for it has become almost a matter of policy. On December 6, 1962, Pentagon information chief, Arthur Sylvester, made the startling statement that "it's inherent in the Government's right, if necessary, to lie, to save itself when it's going up into a nuclear war. This seems to me to be basic." Subsequent to the storm of indignation that greeted this statement, Sylvester disowned it — but in the process of disowning he got into it deeper. Appearing before the Senate Permanent Investigations Subcommittee on March 13, 1963, he declared: "The Government does not have a right to lie to the people, but . . . I think that any people will support their Government in not putting out information that is going to help the enemy. *And, if necessary, misleading them.*"

(Emphasis added.) A former White House press secretary, Robert H. Fleming, said he was opposed to deliberate lying, but "hiding the full truth is sometimes in the interest of national policy." Malcolm Kilduff, assistant press secretary for Presidents Kennedy and Johnson told the Texas Public Relations Association September 9, 1966: "There are times when lying is justified." In moments of high oratory government leaders affirm — as former Vice President Hubert Humphrey did in a 1965 speech at Medford, Massachusetts — that "the first principle of our public morality is that the truth must be told." But the principle keeps clashing with expediency and with the general notion in a militarist era that "we must keep our people united." The public is therefore immunized from the truth through exaggeration, underplaying, secrecy, and many other ways, if the truth is liable to create tensions or misgivings. It isn't confined only to matters of foreign policy; it seems to seep into all kinds of areas.

On the eve of the midterm election of 1966, for instance, White House press secretary Bill Moyers informed newsmen: "The President's health is excellent." Two hours later the President in "excellent" health announced he would soon undergo abdominal and throat surgery.

Late in 1966 NASA officials reviewing Project Gemini, referred to it as "a perfect sequence of events"; there had been 12 Titan lift-offs in 12 tries. Actually, as columnist William Hines reported, there had been 14 Titan tries and two of them had failed.[22]

Two days after President Johnson's inauguration in 1965 press secretary George Reedy told reporters that no agreement had been "concluded as yet" between the President and Vice President Humphrey on how the Government would be run if Johnson were disabled. A short time later when Johnson was hospitalized with a cold, Reedy announced that such an agreement actually was in existence — it had been made "some time before the inauguration."

It would be naive to suggest that the art of prevarication is an innovation of the military-industrial complex. With rare exceptions, here and elsewhere, all governments lie. But deception has been greatly augmented under the militarist *elan* which now pervades our society. "The political lie," observes Walter Cronkite of CBS, "has become a way of bureaucratic life."

Still another feature of the military syndrome that has the effect of ensuring conformity, is the loyalty-security program. Since we seem to be in permanent "war," even in peacetime, it is deemed necessary to assure "loyalty." The Atomic Energy Act of 1946 required a rigorous screening of AEC employees for "character, associations, and loyalty." A year later, President Truman propounded a loyalty program for *all* people in the federal employ. In the first five years thereafter, the FBI, according to J. Edgar Hoover, processed four million applications for government jobs.[23] Soon there was a cascade of measures to check the "loyalty" not only of federal employees, but of those in federal housing projects and in private industry. A million tenants in government-financed homes had to sign loyalty oaths that they were not Communists. Some were evicted for failing to comply. Lieutenant Milo J. Radulovich, whose own loyalty was impeccable, was discharged from the Air Force Reserve because his father read a Slavic-language newspaper which was pro-Communist, and his sister associated with "Communist fronts."[24] A New York policeman was dismissed because he signed a petition for a Communist candidate for the city council. Before long loyalty oaths were being required of teachers in grammar schools and professors at universities, maritime workers and workers in defense factories. In Indiana, boxers and wrestlers had to sign loyalty affidavits before they could fight or wrestle. The Attorney General of the United States prepared a list of 200 "subversive" organizations, many defunct, as a guide for checking the loyalty of federal workers and others.

In the last decade the raucous witch-hunting associated with Senator Joseph McCarthy has passed into limbo. The nation's youth in particular have developed a sense of humor on the subject. But the loyalty-security program is still with us. Like national conscription, which passed the House in 1940 by a single vote and is now accepted unquestioningly by most people, the loyalty-security program is no longer considered abnormal or dangerous. It has passed into the national subconscious almost subliminally. Yet under the five federal loyalty-security programs more than 10 million people are checked by the Pentagon, FBI, and other agencies for their "loyalty."

A former member of the Council of Economic Advisors says that secret reports given him about job applicants included not only political data but details of their sex life. How much this dampens the spirit of dissent among millions of scientists, civil servants, soldiers, workers, and DOD employees cannot be measured. But it is safe to assume that with a sword hanging over their heads many are constrained to be silent on controversial issues in order to protect their jobs.

What we are witnessing in America as a result of the military syndrome is an exacerbation of the "power gap" — greater prerogatives for an elite at the top, sterner manipulation of the great mass at the bottom. Certainly the military-industrial complex did not create this power gap — it has always been with us — but it has widened it perceptibly, and if it pushes it to its logical conclusion it will have forged the political monopoly that social scientists call the "garrison state."

One final feature of the militarist syndrome worth dwelling on is the tendency of the Pentagon to expand, to take over functions and duties in fields far removed from "preparedness." This, too, is part of the logic of militarism, for if we are to be molded into a disciplined people, the disciplining agency — the military — is better equipped to do it, the more civilian functions it assumes.

Here are a few examples of the trend:

Early in 1969 DOD began equipping a multimillion-dollar Army operations center in the Pentagon basement, 400 feet long, 250 feet wide. This was to be a "war room" for the "dispatch and coordination of military troops in the event of urban riots this summer." The center was planned to have a battery of computers, a memory bank, an overhead map rack with 76 sliding panel boards, closed circuit television, hundreds of telephone and radio lines — many of them "secure circuits" — and such sophisticated equipment as an ultrasonic motion detection device to ferret out troublemakers in a protected area.

The center is the result of the Pentagon's quick footwork in seizing opportunity. In 1968, after the outbursts that followed Martin Luther King's assassination, DOD set up a riot control committee to "coordinate activities relating to civil disturbances." It was a small, makeshift operation, with meager staff and a few telephones. Since the Department of Justice has first responsibility for civil disturbances few people expected DOD to move much further in the field. It certainly did not need an elaborate facility to guide 20,000 or 25,000 troops in riot activity. Justice's own "command post," the *Washington Star* reports, was "hardly more than a standard conference room." But the Pentagon had the money and there was no one to say "No," so it went ahead with the new center. In 1968 it was prepared to handle five riots simultaneously; it now boasts a capability of dealing with 25 at once — virtually a revolution.

"Because there is no comparable facility in any other government agency," comments *Washington Star* reporter Robert Walters, "the center will probably become the focus of all federal efforts to cope with large scale urban disorders."[25]

Another new function added to DOD's firmament early in 1969 was the formation of a Domestic Action Council. Three months before he left office, former Secretary Clark Clifford told the twenty-fifth annual dinner of the National Security Industrial Association: "I believe that we in the Department of Defense have not only a moral obligation but an opportunity to contribute far more to the *social needs* of our country than we have ever done before." (Emphasis added.) For those who raised an eyebrow at the idea of the military doing something about "social needs," Clifford explained that the Pentagon was uniquely fitted by experience to dabble in this area. Take housing, he said. The average contractor does 50 units a year at a high cost per unit because his operation is small and he lacks know-how. That's why, Clifford continued, low-cost housing for the unskilled "is so unattractive to private enterprise. There are not enough incentives to justify an entrepreneur risking his limited capital."

Slums, therefore, perpetuate themselves. "What is clearly needed are new materials and new production techniques that will make low-income housing a profitable enterprise." That, Clifford said, was where DOD comes in. It spends $200 million a year for new construction, plus $450 million for maintenance and operation of existing buildings. With its expertise it can initiate a research and development program, and help solve the problem. The exact form of this collaboration with private enterprise was left vague, but Clifford envisioned it not only for housing, but for education, schools, hospitals, health. "We now have a military-industrial team," he pointed out, "with unique resources of experience, engineering talent, management, and problem-solving capacities, a team that must be used to help find the answers to complex domestic problems as it has found the answers to complex weapons systems."[26] Exactly how these notions will be implemented is not yet known, but the present secretary, Laird, is reported to be "enthusiastic" about the prospects.

Wherever it has a foothold, the Pentagon tries to expand outward. Consider foreign affairs. In theory, relations with foreign nations are the sole responsibility of the Department of State. In practice, the wishes of DOD can seldom be bypassed, in part because it is represented on the National Security Council and interagency committees, and in part because it has military attachés around the world and, as of 1967, 4,618 agents operating military assistance programs. There is also the matter of military bases and installations abroad, which State must consider when negotiating with foreign states. One of the items on the agenda when talks were being held with the Filipinos about independence, for instance, was the vaunted air and naval bases which the War Department insisted remain in American hands. Similarly State must be sensitive to the Pentagon's views on foreign trade and raw materials. A dispatch in *The New York Times* many years ago, but still applicable, asserts that the armed services have been represented at all "major international trade conferences to 'see that the interests of national defense are fully considered in determining the trade policy of the United States.' "[27] A *Washington Post* article by Warren Unna (June 29,

1969) reports that "there has been a behind-the-scenes struggle within the administration over liberalizing restrictions on trading with communist Europe, and the President has now sided with the military against any such liberalization. Since trade, more than most subjects, is definitely within the realm of foreign affairs and the State Department's jurisdiction, it would appear that the Pentagon has been assigned some new responsibilities."

A barometer of the foreign policy role of the military is the fact that for fiscal 1968 DOD budgeted $27 million "on foreign policy-oriented research and nearly $40 million on research in foreign countries. At the same time the intelligence and research operation of the Department of State will spend only $5 million."[28] Among the items researched at DOD's expense were the political influence of university students in Latin America, "Witchcraft, Sorcery, Magic and Other Psychological Phenomena" in the Congo, alternative strategies for insurgent conflicts, political development and revolutionary behavior, ideology and behavior, resettlement in Latin America. None of this appears to have any relevance to waging war, but the Pentagon's vistas keep widening with opportunity. Anyway, as Fulbright observed to DOD's Dr. Foster: "You are able to get so much money . . . it (is) superfluous for the State Department or anyone else to attempt to enter this area of research."[29]

The Pentagon thus adds the new function of "peacefare." A Defense Science Board panel in 1967 summed it up succinctly:

> The DOD mission now embraces problems and responsibilities which have not previously been assigned to a military establishment. It has been properly stated that the DOD must now wage not only warfare but "peacefare" as well. Pacification assistance and the battle of ideas are major segments of the DOD responsibility.

If "peacefare," "domestic action," and policing against riots are added to the Pentagon's jurisdiction its responsibilities verge on the infinite. Yesterday the earth, today the moon, tomorrow the universe.

CHAPTER FIVE

Self-fulfilling Strategies

While on a trip around the world in the summer of 1969, President Nixon pledged, as *The New York Times* paraphrased, "that the United States would not be enticed into future wars like the one in Vietnam." The pledge was enigmatic, as indicated a few days later when Nixon reaffirmed to Thai Premier Thanom Kittikachorn America's commitment to help its allies against domestic insurgents.[1] Even so, it had a pleasant ring for most American ears because the President attached two provisos to U.S. aid — first, that it would be forthcoming only to the extent that a beleaguered government was ready to help itself, and second, that in no circumstances would American troops do any actual fighting. The chief executive seemed to be reversing the policy of his four postwar predecessors — in Korea, Lebanon, Vietnam, and the Dominican Republic. His words implied, to a nation disenchanted by the war in Southeast Asia, "no more Vietnams," "no more military interventions."

The obvious question critics are bound to ask, however, is: Can you apply the brakes while gunning the motor? Can the United States equip, advise, encourage allies like Thailand, without walking the last mile to actual combat?

Other Presidents have expressed similar nonintervention policies, but somehow the nation has overstepped the bounds. During Harry Truman's tenure, for instance, the United States

negotiated a treaty with all of Latin America, forbidding unilateral intervention in unmistakable language. Article 15 of the
Charter of the Organization of American States proclaims
categorically that "no State or group of States has the right to
intervene, directly or indirectly, for any reason whatever, in the
internal or external affairs of any other State. The foregoing
principle prohibits not only armed force, but also any other form
of interference. . ."[2] The treaty, however, was no monumental
barrier to intervention in Cuba and the Dominican Republic, or
the many indirect interventions by the CIA in Guatemala, Brazil,
Bolivia, and a half dozen other hemispheric nations where military
coups were on the agenda.

President Kennedy expressed an identical position to that of
President Nixon six years before. Apropos of Vietnam, he said
in 1963 that "in the final analysis it's their war. . . . We can help
them, give them equipment, we can send our men there as advisors, but they have to win it."[3] On August 12, 1964, President
Johnson told the nation — again on Vietnam:

> Some others are eager to enlarge the conflict. They call upon us to
> supply American boys to do the job that Asian boys should do. They
> ask us to take reckless action which might risk the lives of millions
> and engulf much of Asia and certainly threaten the peace of the entire
> world. Moreover, such action would offer no solution at all to the real
> problem of Vietnam.[4]

But these words were no obstacle to escalation. As of the end
of 1964, the South Vietnamese government was crumbling, and,
faced with this prospect, Johnson did begin the bombing of North
Vietnam, and did send troops to do the fighting in South Vietnam
that he said Asian boys should be doing.

Cynics may question the integrity of America's chief executives
in the light of this record, but there are sound political explanations for the gap between rhetoric and action that need not be so
Machiavellian. Every government prefers to gain its objectives
through diplomatic means, rather than war; it is much cheaper,
much less disturbing to the populace. But if it is prepared with
mighty armies and weapons to use military force "in case of an

emergency," the emergency always seems to crop up. As theologian Reinhold Niebuhr observed many years ago, "it is the business of military strategists to prepare for all eventualities, and it is the fatal error of such strategists to create the eventualities for which they must prepare."[5] Given the objectives for which the military-industrial complex was formed — to secure bases around the world, to contain enemies with "regimented economies," to protect allies with "free economies" who favor U.S. trade and investment — given these objectives, it must be ready to handle scores of eventualities in scores of countries.

As of 1964, the United States was supplying weapons to 69 nations, half the sovereign states in the world. Since then the figure has been cut by congressional edict, but it is safe to say that DOD has contingency plans in its files, as well as maps and intelligence, equipping it to fight in any of these places on the shortest notice.[6] That includes evidently not only direct military action but what has been called "peacefare" as well. There was a furor in the summer of 1965 when a secret Army study called Project Camelot was brought to light.[7] The project, undertaken by American University beginning in 1962, focused on "turmoil-ridden areas," such as Chile, Quebec, Brazil, and at least a dozen others, with a view toward influencing their internal politics. A Chicago labor expert was approached by an American University professor and asked to prepare a plan for the Army on "how to deal with the Brazilian labor movement if a state of insurgency should develop there." Many Americans were outraged by Project Camelot, but it wasn't as far-fetched as it appeared. If the Army must contemplate participating in a war in Brazil, it must also have plans for dealing with the Brazilian labor movement if it should decide to call a general strike.

With strategies worked out in such detail and with the forces at hand to implement them it is virtually inevitable that there will be a few occasions when the American government, whatever the rhetoric of its leaders, will be carried across the brink to actual combat. C. Wright Mills may have been simplistic when he prophesied in 1958 that "the immediate cause of World War III is the preparation for it," but there is a large element of truth to what he said.[8] The mere availability of plans and weapons is a temptation to use them. It may be a temptation which is acceded to in a minority of instances, but it is enough to make the preparation for war an independent factor in creating it.

An example that illustrates this thesis occurred during the prelude to the Bay of Pigs fiasco. In 1960 the CIA, with Pentagon support, was training a Cuban exile force in a remote town of Guatemala called Retalhuleu. Neither the American nor the Guatemalan people had any knowledge that there was such a camp or what was going on there. It had been acquired in a secret arrangement with President Miguel Ydigoras, a former general on excellent terms with Washington, and it had been expected that no one would discover its existence until after the invasion of Cuba had taken place.

But on November 13 part of the Guatemalan army rebelled against the Ydigoras regime and seized Puerto Barrios, a banana port on the Caribbean. This presented a problem for American planners at Retalhuleu, for if the friendly government should fall the new one that would replace it might cancel the training camp arrangement and the invasion of Cuba might have to be postponed for months, or even scrapped. The dilemma was resolved by dispatching American B-26s, with Cuban and American pilots, to bomb the airport at Puerto Barrios. C-46s were used to transport loyal Ydigoras troops to the scene, and in short order the rebellion was suppressed. Perhaps, if Congress or the American public had had a choice in the matter they might have opted to let the Guatemalan dictator sink. But Congress was never informed of these developments; in effect the CIA and the Pentagon were making their own foreign policy. The weapons were at hand — why not use them?[9]

Would the United States have shipped 27,000 troops to the Dominican Republic in April 1965 if the forces were not available and if the Pentagon didn't have a plan for just such an emergency? Would American Marines have been landed in Beirut, Lebanon in July 1958? Would there have been a war in Korea or Vietnam if a vast military establishment was not ready — perhaps eager — to meet such eventualities?

In an article on "The New American Militarism," former Marine Commandant General Shoup gives us a rare behind-the-scenes look at the Pentagon operation. In addition to plans for "defense against actual direct attack on the United States" and for nuclear deterrence, he says, the military "deploys certain forces to forward zones . . . and maintains an up-to-date file of scores of detailed contingency plans which have been thrashed out and approved by the Joint Chiefs of Staff." From this point there ensues "intense rivalries between the Navy-Marine sealift forces and the Army-Air Force team of air-mobility proponents." Each arm of the military wants to prove in action that it can do the job quicker and better than the other. "The danger presented by this practice," says Shoup, "is that readiness and deployment speedily become ends in themselves." They tend to supersede diplomacy. Before "the world realized what was happening, the momentum and velocity of the military plans propelled almost 20,000 U.S. soldiers and Marines" into the Dominican Republic, and in Vietnam the same year where "the four services were racing to build up combat strength . . ."[10] Ironically, the last time the United States had intervened with armed force in any Latin American country was in 1925 when Calvin Coolidge sent the Marines into Nicaragua to suppress a liberal revolt against a conservative, much as Johnson did in Santo Domingo 40 years later.[11]

Sending the Marines all too often seems to be the easiest solution when the Marines are available. On May 12, 1958 an armed rebellion broke out in Beirut against President Camille Chamoun, who had rigged the elections of 1957 and seriously divided the country. In the ensuing turmoil an American library was burned down by demonstrators and an oil pipeline was cut. Chamoun, Washington's ally, immediately appealed to the United States to save him, and Secretary of State John Foster Dulles received Eisenhower's permission to dispatch troops when he saw fit. The U.S. temporized for a while because of dissension within the administration, but when a revolt broke out in oil-rich Iraq shortly thereafter and overthrew the regime of Nuri Said, Washington gave the marching orders. The Marines were sent into Beirut and the American ambassador to Iraq was advised by the State Department, according to columnist Jack Anderson, "that the U.S. Marines, starting to land in Lebanon, might be used to aid loyal Iraqi troops to counterattack." Fortunately or unfortunately, no "loyal Iraqi troops" came forth to ask for U.S. help, and the venture remained limited.[12]

In far more instances than the American public realizes, the militarist orientation of American policy and the easy access to military forces carries the United States to the water's edge of intervention. In April 1964, by way of example, there was a coup d'etat by General Humberto Castelo Branco in Brazil against the elected government of João Goulart. The United States had been quite unhappy with Goulart: he had permitted the nationaliza-tion of the American and Foreign Power Company and the Brazil-ian Telephone Company, had restricted the remittance of profits by foreign corporations, was buying crude oil from the Soviet Union, and had invited a delegation from China to discuss trade relations. He was talking of giving illiterates the right to vote (still denied to them), of land reform and other social changes, and was encouraging rank-and-file soldiers and sergeants in the armed forces who were forming clubs against the military hier-archy. At the time of the Castelo coup the nation was beset with strikes, demonstrations, turmoil in the Army and what have you; had Goulart called on the people, as well as some of his sup-porters in the Air Force and Army, to rebel, there probably would have been a major civil war in Brazil. But he elected to flee with-out a battle.

Subsequently, reputable Brazilian newsmen learned from the governors of São Paulo and Minas Gerais (the two most im-portant states in the country) that the United States had offered them substantial military aid in case of civil conflict. Governor Carlos Lacerda of Guanabara, an original participant in Castelo's coup who broke with it later, publicly confirmed that he too had been approached by the U.S. and promised all the help needed if he would declare a "state of belligerency" against the Goulart government. What makes this saga more ominous was the fact that while the coup was taking place American naval units were offshore near Rio de Janeiro. When American reporters asked the Pentagon what they were doing there, they were told they were at hand to evacuate U.S. citizens if necessary — the same line that Lyndon Johnson was to take a year later when naval units neared Santo Domingo. It doesn't require too much imagination to visualize what might have happened if full-scale civil war had broken out; the same slow process of intervention and escalation might have followed as in Vietnam or the Dominican Republic — and Brazil is 85 million people and incomparably larger than Vietnam.[13]

In carrying out the mandate for "preparedness" the Pentagon has elaborated strategy on two fronts. Its "strategic forces" are designed to deter a nuclear attack and to fight an all-out nuclear war if necessary. Its "general purpose forces" are programmed to fight "two and a half wars" *simultaneously*: a NATO war in Europe, a war against China in Southeast Asia, and a minor war in Latin America such as the Dominican Republic.[14]

The two and a half war policy is not secret. Secretaries of Defense refer to it constantly in their annual posture statements. But given the remarkable disposition in Congress to give the Pentagon what it wants, the policy has never been seriously questioned. The American public has never weighed alternate plans for, say, a two-war or a one-and-a-half-war preparedness program. It has simply assumed that we *must* prepare for two and a half wars at the same time because the Pentagon has said so. As a consequence, DOD has plans for meeting virtually any "emergency" anywhere, and the weapons to match.

No one can reassemble the facts of history to prove that a certain event or series of events might not have occurred under other circumstances, but there will always be a lurking feeling that many of the crises in the world during the last quarter of a century would have been resolved otherwise, and without military means, if the Pentagon were not there with its guns and troops. By way of further example: The Shah's coup against Premier Mohammed Mossadegh in Iran, 1954, was "about to collapse" when the U.S. Military Assistance Mission — according to its director, Major General George C. Stewart — began supplying "the [Iranian] army . . . on an emergency basis —

blankets, boots, uniforms, electric generators, and medical supplies," as well as the hardware of war. It was these supplies and American guns, trucks, armored cars, and radio communication equipment, General Stewart boasted, that made it possible to overthrow "a government unfriendly to the United States."[15]

In October 1962, while United Nations units strove to re-create order in the Congo (Léopoldville), Uncle Sam's forces took matters into their own hands. Instead of letting the U.N. handle the problem as it was established to do, a hundred American military personnel began training and supplying Congolese troops. CIA assigned a few American flyers for combat missions and a dozen Congolese officers were brought to Fort Knox, Kentucky, to learn the fine art of counterinsurgency. When three revolts broke out in 1964 and rebel forces captured Stanleyville, the American government plunged deeper into the morass. U.S. transport planes flew in 540 Belgian paratroopers to Stanleyville with the twin purpose of rescuing 218 Belgian and 16 American hostages — as well as overthrowing the rebel regime. Holding hostages, of course, is a nasty business, and it is understandable that Belgium and the United States should have wanted them freed. The hostages were taken, however, only to force Premier Moise Tshombe to stop the bombing of Stanleyville, and certainly would have been released without much ado had it ended. Richard J. Barnet, a former official with the arms control agency, writes:

There is little doubt from [Ambassador William] Attwood's own account that had the United States ordered Tshombe to stop bombing Stanleyville, the U.S. and Belgian hostages would have been released. It is equally clear that the prime objective of U.S. policy in the Congo in 1964 was to bring down the Gbenye regime because of its reckless character and radical orientation.[16]

Here, in embryo, are the makings of other Vietnams. The U.S. gives military and logistical support to a "friendly" government to help it stay in power. If that is enough to defeat the rebels, as in the Congo or Iran, the matter ends there. If it isn't, as in Vietnam or the Dominican Republic, the pressure is to go further. We send in economic aid to Ngo Dinh Diem's South Vietnam, then some university experts to train and arm his palace guard and police, then a few advisors for his army, and when more is needed 22,000. Finally, all of this having failed to hold off the insurgents, the American government takes over most of the actual fighting and bombing.

A Pentagon lecturer at one of its national security seminars lists four "U.S. options in insurgency situations":

1. Military advice and assistance to the country's military establishment.
2. Training by American officers and enlisted men.
3. Adequate and suitable material for this kind of war.
4. If necessary, direct support by U.S. forces of combat missions launched by government troops, and *unilateral U.S. operations against the insurgents.*[17]

In the Congo the fourth step did not have to be taken because the rebels were unable to continue fighting. It may be that President Johnson, already plagued by Vietnam, would have shied away from it anyway. The point is that the Pentagon was ready, and the temptation was there. In many cases the government found it unnecessary or undesirable to yield to that temptation. In a few — Vietnam, the Dominican Republic, Lebanon, Korea — on the other hand, it proved irresistible. Whether President Nixon can now withstand military enticements that other Presidents (and he as Vice President) could not, is a matter of speculation. The temptation will certainly be strong in Thailand — despite the President's pledge — if the guerrilla war in the Northeast should spread nationwide. Conceivably the administration can even be lured into the maelstrom in Falangist Spain. That the thought has occurred to the Pentagon is evidenced by revelations in the summer of 1969 that U.S. troops had engaged in two major joint maneuvers with Franco's forces and a number of minor ones "to practice suppressing a theoretical rebellion against the Spanish government."[18]

It does not seem consistent for the White House to talk about "no more Vietnams," while the Department of Defense calls for continued production of C-5A planes capable of carrying large numbers of American troops anywhere in the world, fast Navy ships capable of supplying them, and 15 aircraft carriers (the Russians have none) capable of giving them air and naval cover. "The danger of such forces," Senator Fulbright told the Proxmire subcommittee, "is that we will be tempted to use them if we have them and to intervene anywhere in the world if trouble breaks out."[19]

The situation is complicated by two other factors: (1) The Pentagon doctrine of "victory," and (2) technological pressures for producing ever more sophisticated weapons.

It is understandable that an institution charged with the management of war should formulate plans for winning them. The object of war is "victory," General Douglas MacArthur was wont to say. But "winning" has a different connotation for generals than, say, for diplomats. It implies total defeat and surrender by the enemy, and it leads the militarists into a nether world where vestiges of morality and restraint disappear. The "kill" statistic becomes a mark of excellence, to the point where the method by which the kill was achieved becomes almost irrelevant. Even deaths on our own side are contemplated in terms more statistical than human.

A small accident in the summer of 1969 unwittingly disclosed that the United States was storing lethal gas in Okinawa, West Germany, South Korea, and perhaps elsewhere abroad. Twenty-four American soldiers were incapacitated in Okinawa when nerve gas began to escape from its cylinders. Fortunately no one was killed. When pressed for an explanation by Japan, the United States verified the fact that the gas had indeed been placed on the island base, as well as in other parts of the world. It had been put there, said Daniel Z. Henkin, Pentagon public affairs secretary, as a *routine* matter in line with political decisions taken in 1961 and 1963.[20] What was its purpose? The Pentagon took the Fifth Amendment, but very likely the gas was deployed in Okinawa as part of a contingency plan should the war in Vietnam escalate further or spill over into China. In any case, DOD, in seeking "victory," was obviously less inhibited by the many international treaties against lethal gas or the strong public opinion against it, than it should have been. Even in World War II the United States had refrained from such weapons, and during the Korean War, it denied vehemently, as the Communists charged, that it had used them. Yet it was there in Okinawa, on the ready, and no one can be sure whether it would have been employed or not if the opportunity had presented itself.

More serious is the disposition to toy with nuclear weapons. Americans generally assume that these instruments of mass horror are meant simply to *deter* the Russians and Chinese; they will really never be utilized. On more than one occasion American Presidents have said that the United States will never be the first to drop a nuclear bomb. The thought of either initiating or provoking new Hiroshimas and Nagasakis frightens even some of the most audacious — at Hiroshima 78,000 were killed by one bomb and 84,000 injured; at Nagasaki 27,000 killed and 41,000 wounded.[21]

Nonetheless the U.S. government or its military arm has seriously considered the employment of nuclear weapons in a number of critical situations. In 1954 when the French forces were reeling in Indochina, French Foreign Secretary Georges Bidault discussed the problem with U.S. Secretary of State Dulles. On two occasions, Bidault told authors Roscoe Drummond and Gaston Coblentz, Dulles offered France:

the use of American atomic bombs. . . . The first is recalled by Bidault as an offer of one or more atomic bombs to be dropped on communist Chinese territory near the Indochina border in a countermove against the Chinese supply lines to the Viet Minh Communists. The second is recalled as an offer of two atomic bombs against the Viet Minh forces at Dienbienphu.[22]

Another plan reviewed with eight congressional leaders by Dulles and chairman of the Joint Chiefs, Admiral Arthur Radford, was the dispatch of 200 planes from two Navy carriers and the Phillipines to conduct a single mass bombing to relieve Dienbienphu.[23] A number of writers claim that Radford intended to arm these planes with tactical atomic bombs.[24] It was only because the legislators (including Lyndon Johnson) were cool to the plan, and Britain refused to endorse it, that President Eisenhower scrapped it.

In September 1966, almost a decade and a half after the Korean War had slithered to an inconclusive finish, Dwight Eisenhower revealed that he had threatened to use nuclear bombs to force a compromise. "I let it be known," he said, "that if there was not going to be an armistice . . . we were not going to be bound by the kind of weapons that we would use. . . . I don't mean to say that we'd have used those great big things and destroyed cities, but we would use them enough to win and we, of course, would have tried to keep them on military targets, not civil targets."[25] The former President would not say that the United States should ever conduct a massive nuclear attack on the Soviets — except in retaliation — but "this does not mean that in sticky situations that you couldn't use a proper kind of nuclear weapon sometime. I just don't see any difference between gas warfare and this kind of warfare."

Theodore Sorensen, President Kennedy's chief aide, informs us in his biography of the assassinated leader, how the Joint Chiefs reacted to the Laotian crisis of 1961. To put pressure on the Pathet Lao for a cease-fire, they recommended as a first step landing conventional troops in Thailand and South Vietnam. If that failed, the Joint Chiefs proposed "an air attack on Pathet Lao positions and tactical nuclear weapons on the ground. If massive Red troops were then mobilized, nuclear bombings would be threatened and, if necessary, carried out. If the Soviets then intervened, we should be 'prepared to accept the possibility of a general war.' " All this, mind you, to force a cease-fire in a little known land called Laos![26]

That same year, 1961, there was a crisis over Berlin and the lights were burning low both at the White House and the Pentagon to work out a strategy to meet it. Everyone agreed, Arthur Schlesinger, Jr. tells us, "that a Soviet blockade of West Berlin would have to be countered first by a Western thrust along the Autobahn." General Lauris Norstad, the supreme commander of NATO, and others, however, insisted that the probe be undertaken solely "to create a situation where the West could use

nuclear weapons." Conventional weapons and armies, said Norstad, were too expensive and might not result in victory anyway. Hydrogen bombs were a much better response.[27]

The Cuban missile crisis of October 1962, of course, brought
the nation as close to an all-out nuclear war as it ever has been.
Had it broken out, Kennedy said, there would have been 80
million dead Americans within a few hours no matter who pressed
the button first. This time the meetings of an enlarged National
Security Council in the White House cabinet room and elsewhere
were more grim. The choice boiled down to three alternatives:
to overlook the incident and do nothing, blockade Cuba and
"maintain the options," or attack the missile sites on the island
immediately. The decision was eventually made for the blockade, but not before, as Robert Kennedy recorded in a posthumous
article, "one member of the Joint Chiefs argued that we could
use nuclear weapons. . ." As he listened, the younger Kennedy
thought "of the many times that I had heard the military take
positions which, if wrong, had the advantage that no one would
be around at the end to know."[28]

The Kennedy brothers evidently were the moderates during
the missile crisis, compared to those who were ready to start
dropping nuclear bombs without ceremony. But it is a testament
to the fragile logic of a militarist era that John Kennedy could
say at the height of the crisis that if war were to break out "even
the fruits of victory would be ashes in our mouth" — and then
add: "but neither will we shrink from that risk at any time it
must be faced."[29]

The willingness to gamble with the idea of nuclear war, even
when "victory" would simply mean "ashes," indicates a loss of
touch with reality, almost a suicidal impulse. The militarists are
not unaware of this problem. They use the word victory in dealing with counterinsurgency wars, but they are sometimes hesitant
when referring to nuclear combat. Often they speak of achiev-
ing an "equilibrium," and they elaborate scenarios of minimum
wars (as opposed to maximum) in which each side will be
sufficiently disciplined to drop a few bombs and then *stop*. At
other times they throw caution to the winds and speak of out-

right victory, by which they mean "killing more of them than they kill of us." In either case the *preparation* must be — under Pentagon theorems — not for a minimum but a maximum war; and the very preparation brings on situations that can explode into actual nuclear war.

Consider the 1962 missile confrontation again. Everyone was sure a few years ago that it was provoked by the Soviets when they placed missile sites in Cuba. But there are some experts who now lay at least part of the blame on the Pentagon. "There are more than a few people in Washington, around at the time [1962]," writes Morton Kondracke of the *Chicago Sun-Times*, "who believe that the U.S. never would have got into the crisis in the first place had it not been for McNamara's rattling our rocket superiority and implying that the United States intended to use it. . ."[30] At a university commencement a few months before the emergency, Defense Secretary McNamara announced that American strategy was no longer to aim missiles at Soviet cities, where tens of millions would be killed, but at "the enemy's military forces." This was euphemistically called a "city-sparing" strategy. But humane as it sounds, writes Kondracke, such a "targeting doctrine implies that the United States would have to strike first." For there is no sense to fling weapons at Soviet missile sites *after* their missiles are discharged and their silos empty. It only makes sense if you "beat them to the punch."

In the strange gymnastics of nuclear strategy, targeting at the enemy's cities is actually a defensive stance — what is called a *second* strike posture — a "deterrent," a warning to the enemy that if he strikes first he will suffer a fearful retaliation which will cost millions of urban lives. On the other hand, targeting at missile sites is a *first* strike posture, connoting that the Pentagon intends to make a surprise attack to wipe out the Soviet arsenal before it can be used. This was the way Nikita Khrushchev understood the "city-sparing" strategy, according to those who are reviewing the situation, and it resulted, says Kondracke, in the Russian decision to "harden" its missile bases (make them less vulnerable), as well as to emplace intermediate-range missiles in Cuba.

Planning to win drives the Pentagon to ever-wider flights of fancy for ultimate security and the ultimate weapon. Nuclear bombs were originally considered solely as a deterrent; they were too horrifying to use, they were deployed only to create a "balance of terror" whereby neither of the superpowers would dare attack each other. General Eisenhower, in that bygone era, warned that "war has become not just tragic but preposterous. With modern weapons there can be no victory for anyone." General MacArthur said it "has become a Frankenstein to destroy both sides . . . double suicide."

But in recent years the Pentagon has adopted another goal — to win. Winning means "to insure that the United States and its allies emerge with relative advantage irrespective of the circumstances of initiation, response, and termination."[31] The new strategy as explained by General Earle G. Wheeler, chairman of the Joint Chiefs, to the Senate Preparedness Subcommittee, goes under the ironic title of "damage-limitation." As things stand, the Soviets have an "assured-destruction" capability to kill 100 million Americans, "give or take 20 million," no matter who pushes the first button. But if their "assured-destruction" capability could be reduced, and our "assured-destruction" capability could be increased beyond 100 million we could survive a nuclear war, while they didn't. To limit damage the United States must be prepared to *strike first*, knocking out the Soviet missile sites *before* their weapons take off — insofar as possible — and must develop a defense, such as ABM and shelters, that will reduce death and destruction to tolerable levels when the Russians retaliate. Wheeler's strategy encompasses a host of new *offensive* weapons, such as MIRV and AMSA (advanced manned strategic aircraft), capable presumably of destroying many more Soviet missile sites than present weapons can; and defensive systems, such as ABM, that will intercept some of the missiles that escape the first strike before they hurtle onto our terrain. And by putting the American people into underground shelters, the human "damage" can also be decreased further. Thus, while we cannot escape with as "few" casualties as we did in World Wars I and II, Wheeler hopes we can come out so much better off than the enemy that the U.S. can continue as a nation, while the Soviet Union disappears. Scores of millions would die but America would survive as a viable society.

When the subcommittee counsel asked Wheeler if the two superpowers had not arrived at a plateau where neither side would "dare to use its strategic nuclear weapons under any circumstances," the general rejected the idea. "I do not think," he said, "we have reached that stage, nor do I think we will necessarily reach it if we exert our brains and if we have the will not to permit it to happen."

Suppose then, he was queried further, that the number of potential deaths in the United States were doubled to 160 million and for the Soviets 200 million. "Obviously," said the subcommittee questioner, "you would have no country left, neither of us." Would the game, then, still be worth the candle? Wheeler snapped back: "I reject the 'better Red than dead' theory — lock, stock, and barrel." There is a certain bewildering ambiguity here between a strategy that is geared to win and yet is willing to see total destruction, but that does not inhibit the military from proceeding full speed ahead with the quest for victory.

Senator Richard B. Russell, one of the Pentagon's closest friends, puts the damage-limiting theory picturesquely: "If we have to start all over again with Adam and Eve, then I want them to be Americans and not Russians, and I want them on this continent and not in Europe."

Herman Kahn, the most imaginative "damage-limiter" — with more influence at the Pentagon than liberals concede — has outlined a scenario for a "war of competitive mobilization" which is the ultimate in the win strategy. Under his plan the United States would declare war, but hold off its attack for a year or two while it built "a spare United States" underground, complete with factories, homes, transport, and what have you. It would cost "hundreds of billions of dollars a year" but, when completed, the Pentagon could plunge into nuclear battle, secure in the knowledge that our death toll would be many millions of people less than that of the enemy. While Kahn has admitted that this is somewhat visionary and may be hard to sell, his fertile brain projects a situation in the future where lasers may be formed into an "anti-ballistic bubble" over the whole country, capable of destroying any Soviet missile that approaches. In this circumstance damage would be limited to the point where nuclear war would, presumably, be "thinkable." Wild as such ideas may sound to the average citizen, they mesh with official Pentagon dogma — that we must plan to win, not merely seek a stalemate, or coexistence, or deterrence.

The Defense Department, of course, would deny that it intends to *start* a nuclear war, and in a strict sense it doesn't — it only wants to be *prepared* to start one. But if it is so prepared, and is targeting its missiles both at Soviet and Chinese cities *and* missile sites, who can say in what emergency the temptation to strike will not become overpowering? A nation might back off from military response if it feels it cannot win. But what if its military leaders believe that it *can* win — albeit through "damage-limitation"?

Where the desire to win is buttressed by the genius of technology the dangers escalate a few notches higher. As far as the eye can see into the distant future the military-industrial complex is leading us to one more wonder weapon after another. Alain C. Enthoven, former Assistant Secretary of Defense for systems analysis, says that the Pentagon program assumes a "greater-than-expected threat"; in other words that the Soviets will develop "their forces to a degree we believe is only remotely possible."[32] General Wheeler makes it clear that DOD wants to proceed with development and deployment of a number of new strategic systems that would cost more than $100 billion in the next 10 or 15 years.[33] Each wonder weapon may be expected to elicit a response from the Soviets or Chinese, and this, in turn, to spur American engineers to develop wonder-wonder weapons.

The atom bomb, with the power of thousands of tons of dynamite, is replaced in half a generation by the hydrogen bomb with the power of millions of tons. The short-range bomber gives way to the intercontinental bomber, and the intercontinental bomber to the unmanned missile carrying a single war-head. The single warhead missile becomes obsolete and is sup-planted by MRV, a missile with three to 15 warheads. Now the spy satellites of the Russians can no longer tell how many war-heads the U.S. has deployed, for they can only picture the missile sites, not the number of bombs on each missile. The Soviets can be expected therefore to begin deploying their own MRVs, and the U.S. to respond with an accelerated MIRV program — a multiple warhead weapon that can *independently* target each bomb to hit a separate missile site or city. Concomitantly the Sprint and the Spartan, as well as new radars, raise hopes that there is, after all, a defense in nuclear war, and so the race con-tinues to find the ultimate weaponry that can assure ultimate victory. There is just no end to the arms race on the present pre-sumptions, especially with thousands of manufacturers breath-ing down the Government's neck trying to get orders for new systems.

Once a system comes off the drawing boards it takes a major miracle to prevent it being deployed, even if its original purpose is no longer tenable. The Poseidon missile for submarines, by way of example, was designed to penetrate the Soviet TALLINN system, then believed to be an anti-*missile* defense. When it was found that TALLINN was far less ambitious — simply an anti-*aircraft* system — the Poseidon might have been discontinued; its raison d'être was gone. Instead, according to Dr. Foster, it was redesigned for more accuracy as a hedge against the new Soviet SS-9s.

Some of the reasoning behind new weapons systems is so far-fetched as to be unbelievable. Charles Schultze, former budget director, gave the Proxmire subcommittee a few examples. The existing SAGE continental air defense system, which cost $18 billion to install, is evidently obsolete because it is "not very effective against low-altitude bomber attack." There is little danger of such a bomber attack, according to the experts, since the Soviets are not concentrating on improving their bombers. But the Pentagon has decided to install a new and better air defense system on the strange thesis that it will deter the Russians from *planning* a better bomber plane. Similarly, the F-14 plane (and its predecessor F-111B) was developed to withstand a Soviet supersonic bomber attack on American aircraft carriers. This threat, the Senate Defense Preparedness Subcommittee said in 1968, was "either limited or does not exist." Yet the program moves ahead. The military mind reasons, in Schultze's words, that "the technology is available — why not use it!"[34] No one in the military-industrial complex seems concerned that each new weapons system impedes disarmament. Indeed neither this nor previous administrations have talked about "disarming" so much as about "arms control" — freezing the weaponry at where it is now, or, possibly, just slowing down the pace of increase.

Nor is this trend toward weapons escalation limited to the nuclear variety. It is also built into the Pentagon's counter-insurgency strategy. One weapon is superseded by another more wondrous one. Most of the generals and admirals are never convinced that wars such as Vietnam or Korea are, at best, stale-mates. There is always a new weapon, which if supplemented by more manpower, freedom of action and a little time is all that is needed to turn the tide toward victory.

Being prepared thus becomes a pressure, a temptation, for being at war. The merry-go-round never stops.

CHAPTER SIX

The Labor Lieutenants

If we may recapitulate the theme of these pages for a moment: The military-industrial complex is not a fateful accident but an outgrowth of a new postwar concept of national purpose — global expansion. The continental expansion of the nineteenth century and the limited imperialism of the first part of this century has widened, as a result of the unparalleled victory in World War II, to global dimensions — demanding for the first time in American history a large military establishment in peacetime.

The domestic backlash of this policy has been to weld together those elitist elements at home which have a stake in militarism — the armed forces, a group of legislators, industrialists, government officials, the labor hierarchy, an important segment of academia — into what Eisenhower called the military-industrial complex. The destiny of that complex, if it is to survive, depends on whether it can mobilize public acceptance of its aims and can fashion a national spirit of discipline and conformity similar to what governments impose, through persuasion and compulsion, in wartime. The result therefore is a specific military syndrome. The military-industrial complex seeks to "manufacture" a public stance of hard-line anti-communism. It withholds information and misinforms the public in critical situations so that the citizenry finds it difficult — sometimes impossible — to make an intelligent assessment of major policies. It inhibits the process of dissent through loyalty and security measures. And it extends its own prerogatives into areas normally reserved for civilians, such as domestic action, riot control, and "peacefare." Taken together, this amounts to a further exclusion of the populace from the decision-making process, especially on issues of war and peace, and a tendency toward *political monopoly*, which is sometimes called the "garrison state." Finally, far from assuring peace, militarism develops a momentum for war. Through military pacts, contingency plans, the utilization of advancing technology, and a crude definition of victory, the very preparation for war has become an independent factor in promoting it.

With this as background, let's turn to the corrupting effects of the military-industrial complex on two milieus that are ordinarily considered liberal and progressive — or at least enlightened: the labor movement and academia. These typify, alas, what is happening to so many segments of our society.

The American labor movement — 18 million strong — has an impressive record, going back to the 1790s, in fighting for the "injured and oppressed." It is responsible in significant measure for many if not most of the nation's social reforms, from free public schools and abolition of imprisonment for debt to social security and unemployment compensation. Its struggles for economic democracy have usually evoked warm sympathy from men of social conscience. But all this is changing.

Early in August 1969 Senator Fulbright and AFL-CIO president George Meany had a surprisingly bitter exchange at a Foreign Relations Committee hearing, which sheds some light on the growing disenchantment of liberals and young radicals with the labor leadership. Fulbright's charge that the Kennedy-Johnson administrations had given the labor federation a $33 million "payoff" for support of the Vietnam War, was called by Meany "a gratuitous insult to the American labor movement." The senator conceded that "payoff" may have been "too strong" in characterizing the payments made by the Agency for International Development (AID) to three institutes under Meany's control, but he would not retreat on the main point: that it was improper for the Government "to provide money to any private organization to go out and influence foreign governments and their parliaments."[1] He also tried to establish that Brazilian graduates of a labor school at Front Royal, Virginia had participated in a military coup against President João Goulart in 1964.

It was not a friendly meeting; at one point the committee chairman accused Meany of rudeness and asked him to stop shouting. The "honest plumber" who runs the AFL-CIO, on the other hand, was clearly piqued by the payoff charge — withdrawn or not — and insisted that the $33 million was used for nothing more than "to carry out the foreign policy of the United States government." He resented the inference that there was anything ignoble in AFL-CIO's international activities. "When the Communists want to take over a country," he said, "they don't bother with the banks or big business and industry. They try to infiltrate and take over the free trade unions." All that the federation was doing was helping those "free unions" to resist communist machinations.

Fulbright and an increasing legion in and out of public office obviously do not agree that Meany and his co-workers are engaged in activities quite so innocent. There is a belated recognition in many places that: (1) The labor hierarchy is a member in good standing of the military-industrial complex, pushing the same hard anti-communist line; and (2) that under the guise of fraternal help it has been involved for a quarter of a century in an overt and covert game of fashioning a foreign labor base for Washington's cold war objectives and counterinsurgency.

The $33 million that has seeped from AID coffers to the American Institute for Free Labor Development (AIFLD), the African-American Labor Center (AALC), and the Asian-American Free Labor Institute (AAFLI), is not a large sum by present standards. Nor are the many millions spent out of the CIA till, and, before CIA, out of other secret funds. But with these sums, and some of its own, the federation has performed a service for the military-industrial complex that none of the other elements in it, including the CIA, could have performed themselves. They have insinuated the Cold War elan into labor institutions of scores of countries; and in a world that has witnessed five dozen national revolutions in two and half decades, this is no small matter. In most countries the labor federations are tied in with one political party or another; strengthening one federation against a rival, therefore, can significantly alter the firmament of power.

Fraternal aid given by the union movement of one country to another — say for an organizing campaign among the unorganized, or for strike relief — is a legitimate labor function that has a long and honorable tradition. But there is a certain point where "fraternal aid" becomes a purposive effort to *buy* a satellite union abroad, and use it as a weapon to alter the foreign policy and power structure of a foreign nation. This indeed is the Meany team's record.

It includes, among many other questionable actions:

1. Helping to split the French and Italian labor movements, as well as others of lesser importance.

2. Encouraging the emergence of conservative leaders in the German unions.

3. Involving themselves in the gathering of hard intelligence.

4. Using strikebreakers and thugs to assure the unloading of American arms in Marseilles and other European ports.

5. Promoting a general strike in British Guiana — with American funds — in an effort to depose the elected Jagan government.

6. Through a satellite union, supporting the overthrow of the Bosch regime in the Dominican Republic.

7. Training Brazilian unionists who helped the generals jettison Goulart.

8. Educating tens of thousands of foreign unionists in their own brand of anti-communism, and setting them loose, with money and other help, to fight native unions with left-of-center leadership.

Beyond this, the AFL-CIO hierarchy has given unqualified support to the arms race, and its fervid stamp of approval to intervention in Cuba, Vietnam, the Congo, the Dominican Republic, as well as lesser counterinsurgency efforts by both the Pentagon and CIA.

The AFL-CIO is made up of 121 affiliates — national unions in various crafts and industries, called "internationals" — and boasts 13.6 million members. In addition there are a number of unions outside the AFL-CIO ranks, the two largest ones being the teamsters' and the auto workers', with a combined membership of more than 3.5 million. Not all of these internationals or their leaders support the Meany policy. Walter Reuther, president of the auto union (UAW), and Frank Fitzsimmons, acting president of the teamsters' (IBT), have recently spoken out against the Vietnam War and the large defense budget. Two years ago a Labor Leadership Assembly for Peace convened in Chicago in open opposition to Meany on these and related issues. Among its 400 participants were nationally prominent figures such as Emil Mazey, secretary-treasurer of UAW; Victor Reuther (Walter's brother); Patrick Gorman, secretary-treasurer of the meat cutters'; Frank Rosenblum, secretary-treasurer of the clothing workers'; Harry Bridges, president of the independent longshoremen; and hundreds of secondary officials. Moreover, the 13.6 million members who belong to AFL-CIO affiliates play absolutely no role in the international projects of AFL-CIO leaders. They do not elect the delegates to the federation's biennial conventions; with rare exceptions those are appointed by the international union officials, who almost invariably choose themselves. Nor are the rank and file or the heads of 70,000 local unions at the grass roots ever given any foreign policy resolutions to discuss in advance. Thus, while Meany undoubtedly speaks for the largest sector of the top AFL-CIO officialdom, his international affairs group is actually an institution in itself, operating on its own mandate.

The key figure below Meany — the man who formulates policy and directs its implementation — is the seventy-one-year-old Jay Lovestone, head of the international affairs department.

The late Edwin Lahey of the *Chicago Daily News* called him "part cloak and suit, part cloak and dagger." Lovestone was one of the founders of the Communist Party after World War I and its general secretary in 1929 when Moscow ordered him expelled. In the three-way fight between Stalin, Trotsky, and Bukharin, he had thrown in his lot with Bukharin and had been disciplined along with his mentor. Once separated from the official Communist Party he formed the Communist Party (Opposition) and for a decade tried to gain readmission to the Communist International. He continued his polemics with the leaders of the American Communist Party, but defended the Soviet Union as a "citadel of labor, showing the workers the real way out of the awful hell of capitalism." Early in the 1940s he dissolved his organization and began the turn toward an anti-communism which today is as fierce as his former anti-capitalism.

Lovestone's closest associate and the key operational figure is Irving Brown. Son of an active teamster, Brown had worked his way through college, participated in various union and unemployed movements, joined with Lovestone in the mid-1930s, and followed him subsequently in the grand conversion. A whirlwind of a man, a self-taught linguist, an indefatigable worker, Brown is an extremely persuasive man when his temper is in control; and in his own way, for his own purposes, quite courageous. Brown has had a variety of assignments under Lovestone and currently guides the African-American Labor Center (AALC). Along with these men must be included Andrew McClellan, once an amateur bullfighter, low-keyed, easy to talk to, and the team's Latin American chieftain; William C. Doherty, Jr., stocky head of AIFLD; Ernest S. Lee, a former Marine major and Meany's son-in-law; Joseph A. Beirne, president of the communication workers' and secretary-treasurer of AIFLD, AALC, and AAFLI; Gerard P. O'Keefe, acting director of the Asian-American Free Labor Institute (AAFLI); and George P. (Phil) Delaney, a special assistant in the State Department, who is the AFL-CIO liaison man. In addition there are the 65 labor attachés in American embassies abroad, who, according to Dan Kurzman of the *Washington Post*, "must always get Lovestone's stamp of approval," plus 150 labor personnel attached to AID missions or working in AID or State Department offices in Washington. If its numbers are not particularly large, it is a formidable machine nonetheless, shaping the views and guiding the actions of union leaders in many countries. It is a machine that does not hesitate to interfere in the internal life of foreign nations on behalf of the cold war policy it shares with the rest of the military-industrial complex.

An extreme example illustrative of this tendency, was the effort to overthrow the government of British Guiana in 1963. Guiana, a small nation with only 600,000 people at the time, was still under British rule, and Cheddi Jagan, an independent Marxist and spokesman for the Indians who form the largest sector of the population, was its prime minister. Since the colony was awaiting independence from the mother country there was much anxiety in Washington and London about a "second Cuba." It was no secret that Washington was applying pressure on London to delay independence until Jagan could be replaced. What seemed like a golden opportunity came when the prime minister introduced a new labor relations law (modeled on the American Wagner Act) which caused fears among Guianese union leaders that they might lose control of the sugar union, largest in the country. They were prepared to call a national strike rather than permit this to happen, and in this situation, writes Neil Sheehan of *The New York Times*, "the Central Intelligence Agency, working under cover of an American labor union" stepped in to give the strike support and direction. "Inspired," as the late Drew Pearson claimed, "by a combination of CIA money and British Intelligence" the ensuing 80-day walkout moved beyond its original scope to the demand that Cheddi Jagan and his party be removed from government.

There were certainly some strange happenings in Georgetown, British Guiana in 1963. For one thing there was an influx of American union officials before and during the strike that, considering the size of the country, was absolutely remarkable. Among them were McClellan, Ernest Lee, Doherty, O'Keefe, Pat Terrill of the steelworkers, William Howard McCabe and Arnold

Zander of the state, county, and municipal union, Gene Meakins of the Newspaper Guild, and four or five others.

According to a secret report by the British police superintendent on the scene — quoted by Susanne Bodenheimer in the *Progressive* (November 1967) — O'Keefe was financing "the activities of the 'security force' (organized gangs) . . . including assassinations and destruction of public buildings with 'explosives and arson.' " Others concentrated on training, advice, and passing out money.

McClellan later recalled to this writer that American labor had contributed about $50,000 to the strike, but a Guianese union official named Pollidor said that strike benefits for 25,000 workers came entirely from American sources, and this amounted to something between $700,000 and $850,000. Jagan claimed the figure was $1.2 million, plus another $2 million for a union housing scheme financed by AIFLD. AIFLD also paid the salaries of six union leaders for the duration of the strike.

If the sums seem small — $700,000 or $1.2 million — they could not possibly have come out of the $10 million annual AFL-CIO budget, and certainly not for so tiny a piece of real estate. What emerges is a strange picture of an American labor hierarchy, using clandestine funds to subsidize a foreign union movement in an effort to jettison its government. The strike failed of this objective but it was an important factor in Jagan's subsequent electoral loss to Forbes Burnham.

Four years later some of the people and organizations involved in this incident admitted receiving CIA money regularly. The Newspaper Guild conceded it had taken a million dollars from CIA foundations. Zander put the sum he obtained from CIA at $12,000 to $15,000 a year, but *New Politics* magazine puts it at $100,000, and "considerably greater sums" for McCabe.

If this cloak and dagger saga seems bizarre, it is not out of character. O. A. (Jack) Knight, former president of the oil workers', is known to have collected large sums from CIA conduits — an ex-CIO official says $10,000 a month — for the petroleum union's activity around the world. When President Johnson in 1967 ordered the CIA to stop the practice of secretly financing student, labor, and similar organizations, AID evidently took over where CIA left off. A May 1968 letter from Ernest Lee to Rutherford M. Poats, deputy administrator of AID, confirms an agreement whereby AID was to channel $1.3 million to AIFLD, AAFLI, and AALC, which in turn was to divide it among seven unions "to obtain their specialized assistance in the international field." Typically, the oil workers' union was asking, as its share, $75,000 each for its activities in Asia and Africa, $100,000 for operations in Latin America, and $50,000 to administer an office in Geneva.[2]

Thomas W. Braden, assistant to CIA chief Allen Dulles from 1950 to 1954, claims that the agency, through him and others, paid out $2 million a year to the Lovestone people for their work in France and Italy alone. His article in the May 20, 1967 *Saturday Evening Post*, "I'm Glad the CIA Is 'Immoral,' " begins:

> On the desk in front of me as I write these lines is a creased and faded yellow paper. It bears the following inscription in pencil: "Received from Warren G. Haskins $15,000 (signed) Norris A. Gambo." . . . I was Warren G. Haskins. Norris A. Gambo was Irving Brown of the American Federation of Labor. The $15,000 was from the vaults of the CIA. . . . (Brown) needed it to pay off the strong-arm squads in Mediterranean ports so that American supplies (weapons) could be unloaded against the opposition of Communist dock workers.

That the CIA was no shy outsider in the labor leadership's international activity is attested to by Victor Reuther. Reuther tells about being called to the American embassy in Paris early in the 1950s, and being asked outright by Braden to become a CIA agent "using as a 'front' his position as European representative of CIO."[3] Reuther declined but he can give you the names of a half dozen labor officials in key posts whom he is confident accepted such offers.

The purpose of all this frenzied spending and recruitment of agents is to create satellite labor movements in much the same way and for much the same purpose as the Pentagon creates satellite armies abroad. George Meany once blandly asserted that "We in the AFL-CIO do not even try to influence the struc-

ture of labor movements in other countries. We teach the fundamentals of union operation; but how the pieces are put together
is up to the people involved."

Clearly this was not the case in British Guiana. Nor has it been
true in Brazil, the Dominican Republic, Bolivia, the Congo,
Nigeria, and many other places. The lavish financing of weak
foreign unions, plus the constant "advice" by American labor
leaders and embassy labor attachés, makes many of these organizations simply conduits for the hard-line anti-communism of
Meany and Lovestone.

Consider, by way of example, the Dominican Republic. The
AFL-CIO's vehicle here is a union federation that goes by the
acronym CONATRAL. In 1963 the regime of Juan Bosch was
under severe pressure by businessmen because it refused to out-
law the Communist Party and refused to denationalize hundreds
of millions of dollars of property seized from the deposed dictator,
Trujillo.

The chorus against Bosch's "softness" on communism was
joined fairly openly by the American military attachés and by
Fred Somerford, the embassy's labor attaché who once served
with the Bureau of Intelligence and Research, as well as CON-
ATRAL. In the critical moment when Bosch needed all the
support he could get, CONATRAL ran a newspaper ad calling
on workers to put their faith in the "armed forces" to restrain
the growing legions of communism. It was jubilant when the
armed forces overthrew Bosch.

Two years later when young military officers tried to reinstate
Bosch, the first democratically elected president in four decades,
CONATRAL was the only one of four labor groups that did not
participate in the popular uprising. The other three federations
of labor accused it of being a "tool of the AFL-CIO, the State
Department, and the Central Intelligence Agency."[4] Instead of
hailing the revolt, CONATRAL, like the AFL-CIO itself, endorsed
American intervention. The AFL-CIO line stated at its 1965
convention, was that "outside intervention in Santo Domingo
was urgent in order to overcome the immediate risk of another
Cuba-type regime . . ."[5]

The role of AIFLD and its trainees in Brazil during the military coup of 1964 seems to have been even more substantial. Doherty, AIFLD's present director, not only supported the coup enthusiastically but boasted that AIFLD graduates "were so active they became intimately involved in some of the clandestine operations" that preceded it. A *Reader's Digest* article of October 1966 states that an AIFLD-trained communication union leader ran seminars in which "he warned key workers of coming trouble and urged them to keep communications going, no matter what happened." When unionists opposed to the coup sent out a call for a general strike "the wires kept humming and the army was able to coordinate troop movements that ended the showdown bloodlessly." Later, hundreds of former AIFLD students were assigned by General Castelo Branco to "reorganize" militant unions whose leaders were ousted by the dictatorship.

Virtually everywhere the AFL-CIO aim is to build a labor base to fight communism and support Washington's friends. A disillusioned former AID official in Bolivia recalls: "By the definition of AIFLD anyone who wanted a raise was a Communist. Its whole purpose was to make the 120 or so men it trained into government supporters. It was willing to do something for union men only if they would kick the Communists out of their union." There existed, he says, a good, legitimate union in the Bolivian railroad industry. But after AIFLD had tutored a small group of railroad workers, the government decided to recognize this new force, led by Sajines Ovando, as the official union. By contrast, the tin miners, Bolivia's largest and most militant organization, were shunned because they were disinclined to support reduction of the work force in the mines and because they had many Communists and Trotskyites in their ranks.

With infrequent exceptions, AFL-CIO policy meshes, as Meany told Fulbright, with that of the U.S. government. Bernard Nossiter of the *Washington Post* has published excerpts from the minutes of a group that meets every two months, called the Labor Advisory Committee on Foreign Assistance.[6]

Chaired by Meany himself, the body includes high officials of AID, the Departments of State and Labor, and the federation.

The minutes of January 8, 1969 record that William Bundy, Assistant Secretary of State for the Far East "thanked Mr. Meany for the strong resolution of support for U.S. policy in Vietnam adopted at the AFL-CIO convention."

The minutes of March 11, 1968 state that "as a result of a request from Secretary Rusk, the AFL-CIO executive council . . . voted to contribute $35,000 . . . to the Vietnamese Confederation of Labor (CVT)." CVT, as might be expected, is the closest labor supporter of the Thieu regime.

The minutes of November 12, 1968 report that Irving Brown has arranged to train drivers for the Nigerian army at an AID-supported drivers' school. "George Meany," comments Nossiter, "for years had condemned unions in communist countries as instruments of government. To some extent at least, American unions have acquired the same image through their relationships with the foreign policy bureaucracies of Washington."

The American labor hierarchy became a segment of the military-industrial complex partly to protect millions of jobs dependent on armaments, partly because of its conservative philosophy. (The CIO, though more liberal and less inclined to act as a government agent, lost its independent role when it merged with the much larger AFL in 1955.)

It all started during World War II with two AFL leaders of divergent origin, David Dubinsky, president of the ladies' garment workers', and Matthew Woll of the photoengravers'. Prior to this period AFL interest in international affairs was minimal. The federation in 1910 did join the International Secretariat of Trade Union Centers, dedicated to "closer association between the trade unions in all countries," to collecting "uniform trade statistics," and to mutual help in "industrial disputes." These purposes were modest enough so that Samuel Gompers, the founder of AFL and its first president, could feel comfortable in ISTUC ranks. But when a successor organization, the International Federation of Trade Unions — the so-called "Amsterdam International" — denounced capitalism after World War I and called for the "socialization of the means of production," the AFL refused to join it. For almost two decades thereafter it confined its internationalist activities to lobbying for higher tariffs to protect some of its constituent unions, and against foreign immigration. Then in 1937 the menace of fascism in Europe and the competition with the CIO at home, drove it temporarily into IFTU ranks. On the whole, however, the AFL's participation in international affairs was remote and of minor importance.

World War II, however, changed all this. The United States was on the verge of becoming the single dominant power in the "free world" and labor's leadership was called on to play a new game. Dubinsky and Woll were strange allies in initiating the project. The peppery head of the garment union, an ex-dress cutter who had once been a socialist, hated the Communists in part as a matter of political doctrine and in part because of internecine war in his own union. Woll, an arch conservative who had once acted as president of the National Civic Federation, an organization of employers and right-wing unionists formed by industrialist Mark Hanna and supplied with money by the Morgans and August Belmont, hated the Communists and radicals generally, because of his intense dedication to capitalism.

Even before the United States entered the war it was obvious to these two men that something had to be done to help old unionists in occupied Europe, since their aid would be useful in winning the war and would be pivotal in rebuilding the continent when the fighting ended. The Labor League for Human Rights which they established in 1940 "for war relief purposes and for support of labor causes everywhere," did provide humanitarian aid for unionists still in the underground or coming out of it. Dubinsky's New York locals raised $300,000 to rescue many of them and keep them in food and shelter. But this was only half the objective, for the other eye was cocked on the communist bogeyman, and as the war drew to a close Dubinsky and Woll, now aided by Meany and William Green, then AFL president, got down to the more serious business at hand. In 1944 they set up the Free Trade Union Committee (FTUC) to revive unions in Europe and Japan and "to help such unions . . . to resist the new drives of totalitarian [i.e. communist] forces."

For executive secretary they chose, ironically, the former head of the Communist Party, Jay Lovestone.

Then in his mid-40s, a vigorous and intelligent man, Lovestone was by all odds an ideal choice. He spoke the language of European Marxists — a language alien to most labor leaders and to the State Department — and he commanded a small band of associates such as Brown, Harry Goldberg, Henry Rutz, equally conversant with left-wing rhetoric and equally committed to save the world labor movement from communism. This was in fact the first contingent of cold warriors, embarked on an anti-communist crusade at a time (1944-47) when the American government still nursed residual hopes of coexisting with the Soviets, and when the Communists themselves were in a remarkably moderate mood.

Before long the planet was covered with old and new Lovestoneites, some on the FTUC payroll, some on that of the AFL, all eager, bright-eyed figures. Rutz was assigned to Germany; Richard Deverall, former executive secretary of the Association of Catholic Trade Unionists, to Japan; Harry Goldberg to Indonesia (later Italy); and Brown virtually everywhere. (According to a laudatory biographer in 1952, Brown had "his fingers in more than 100 individual projects.") The team also included Mrs. Page Morris, an Arab-Muslim expert once an assistant to OSS's Bill Donovan, Maida Springer, Elly Borochowitz, Carmell Offi, and many labor attachés who were "cleared with Jay" before being assigned their posts. Serafino Romualdi, a former Italian socialist who had been picked up by Dubinsky before Lovestone, joined the force independently and carved out a niche as Latin American delegate.

Whatever else may be said of the Lovestone strategy, it was not crude. It rested, as Irving Brown explained in a private interview, on two prongs. First and foremost, the Lovestone group hoped to find capable, "safe," leaders in Europe, Japan, and what is now known as the Third World, to build effective mass movements. Thus, they worked for a while with genuine nationalist revolutionaries, including Ahmed Ben Bella in Algeria and, up to his death, with Patrice Lumumba in the Congo. They also denounced fascist Spain, apartheidist South Africa, and the dictatorships of Paraguay and Haiti, on the theory that such forces offered communism its strongest rationale.

Where the strategy came unstrung, however, was in its back-up plan — if it proved impossible to create strong "safe" trade unions. In that case the Lovestone team was prepared to support almost any measure or force that would defeat communism, including military coups and American intervention. The rationale for this position was an interesting one. As Lovestone now saw it, the world conflict was no mere contest of ideology with the Kremlin, but a permanent war. He disagreed totally with naive liberals who felt that the Soviet bear could be domesticated. All its peace offensives, Lovestone and his friends said, were a fraud. "Throughout its history," as an AFL-CIO executive council meeting in later years expressed it, such offensives were launched only to give the Kremlin "a breathing spell for overcoming difficulties or a pause during which to consolidate its international position and dull the vigilance of the forces opposing it." Everything had to be judged therefore from the focal point of whether it helped or hindered communism. Coexistence was a disaster, and neutralists like the late Jawaharlal Nehru of India, aides-decamp of communism. Neutralism itself was a "conscious or unwitting ally of Soviet imperialism" because it didn't align itself with the United States, the only nation capable of subduing the Soviets.

To their dismay the Lovestoneites found that anti-communism was too weak a reed on which to build great mass movements overseas. There were too many situations in which legitimate goals of laborers had to be sacrificed because fighting for them might help the Communists. For instance, in the mid-1950s the Greek confederation of labor decided to mount a campaign of limited strikes to culminate in a general strike. Brown, according to a private report by a Belgian union leader Walter Schevenels, "tried to dissuade the confederation from undertaking their action. In Brown's opinion the strike action, as contemplated, could not serve any useful purpose. If it failed it would be a disaster and was likely to destroy the confederation. *If it was*

successful, it would only be to the benefit of the Communists."
(Emphasis added.) With this kind of approach one Lovestone-
Brown venture after another ended stillborn — insofar as forging
powerful independent mass movements was concerned — and in
due course the alternative became to support U.S. government
policy, including intervention and counterinsurgency, with little
embellishment. Brown often explained to visitors when he was
stationed in Paris that collaboration with the American government was on the same order as Lenin's willingness in 1917 to
travel in a sealed train through Germany to get back to Russia.
If it were all right for Lenin to accept help from the Kaiser to
fight the Czar, it was all right for Brown and Lovestone to accept
help from Washington to defeat Moscow.

The magic weapon of Brown, Lovestone, and their associates,
apart from strident anti-communist polemic, was and still is
money. A small part came from the AFL (and the AFL-CIO),
the larger part by far from government sources, including the
CIA. Without those tens of millions of dollars the labor dynasty
could not have carried out what it considered to be its cold war
duties. It is probably true that the cold war institutions in the
United States, including the CIA, learned more from Lovestone
and were influenced more by him, than he by them. But without their money, and the willingness of many union officials, who
gained jobs for their men and power for themselves, to give
him a free hand, Lovestone could not have fulfilled what he conceived to be his function. Put crassly, it was to buy labor movements abroad, partly or wholly, in the same way that military
assistance has bought satellite armies.

At any rate, the Lovestone-Meany-Brown policy became one
of disrupting the native labor movement if it were communist-
dominated, and, if the Communists were not yet in charge, to
prevent them from gaining a foothold by pushing anti-Communists to the fore. Often lost in the shuffle were the needs and
desires of the native workers.

The first postwar item on the agenda was to hinder the Krem-
lin-followers from burrowing into the German unions. The
modus operandi was prosaically simple. Europe was digging

out from the shambles of war; everyone was hungry. Union leaders lacked food for their families; offices, typewriters, mimeograph machines, newsprint for their unions. A man who could lay his hands on these items was months, perhaps a year or two, ahead of his rivals. German and other Communists were getting this kind of aid from the Soviet Union; Brown copied the technique for his own — and the American government's — purposes. In Operation Food the AFL leaders sent 5,000 food packages to German unionists of their choice, 15,000 to France, 2,000 to Austria, and 5,000 to Greece. More, the AFL representatives provided equipment, supplies, and cash. By such methods Brown built up a cadre of safe anti-Communists in the German trade unions; he was also helped by the American military government which put restrictions on union activity until it became clear that this "safe" union leadership would emerge in the saddle. Dubinsky was probably right when he wrote in January 1949 that had it not been for the AFL, "the Communists . . . might by now have seized control of the reviving German trade unions."

In France and Italy, where unified labor federations were communist-controlled, Brown's work consisted of artificially splitting the movement. A wave of strikes in May 1947, which Brown's friends denounced as political, offered the excuse for business unionists and mild socialists to withdraw from the General Confederation of Labor. Aging Leon Jouhaux, leader of French labor for many years, opposed the split, insisting it would be better to work within the CGT to win a larger constituency, but he was overruled and carried along. The resulting *Force Ouvriere* was a minor force at birth, its main base in a few white-collar unions, and remains so today. The only thing it did not lack was cash, supplied by Brown from a seemingly inexhaustible stockpile.

The Italian split took a different turn. Here Brown and Harry Goldberg made common cause with the Catholics in the labor movement because the Nenni socialists refused to accept their blandishments and decided to remain with the Communists. In Greece, Brown built a little empire around Fotis Makris, a rightwing politician who took over the unions after the government had purged them of the Communists.

All of this, it should be stressed, went considerably beyond the limits of union-to-union help such as the International Confederation of Free Trade Unions, the non-communist world body of labor, engages in. It is one thing to give a foreign labor organization a few mimeograph machines; it is something else to organize factions within it to split away, and to assure their political reliability by paying a large part of their bills. One case is a justified act of fraternal aid; the other is a brazen interference in the internal affairs of a foreign state. The Swedish Federation of Labor (socialist-oriented) called it a "maniac anti-communist attitude" —"a valuable asset to communism."

In line with this permanent-war-against-communism policy the AFL representatives evidently did not find it inconsistent with their principles to subsidize spying and strikebreaking. Among the organizations whose expenses were being shouldered by Brown was the Free Trade Union Center in Exile in Paris. According to *The New York Times*, October 5, 1947, this organization, with few members, "appears to have at its disposal a working intelligence division." The German railroad union, under Hans Jahn, also seems to have operated a "working intelligence" division. Donald Robinson, a former AFL-staffer who wrote a laudatory piece about Brown for *Reader's Digest*, related that Jahn "told me about an undercover organization he has set up" in East Germany. "Irving Brown helped us."

Particularly distressing for critics like Victor Reuther was Brown's underwriting of what can only be called strikebreaking. In 1949-50 communist trade unionists were refusing to unload American arms at Marseilles. Whether they were right or wrong is beside the point; it was something for *French* labor and the *French* government to decide. But Brown injected himself into this situation foursquare. He subsidized a man named Pierre Ferri-Pisani to form a "Mediterranean committee" for the purpose of getting the weapons unloaded. Thereupon Ferri-Pisani's hired thugs beat up, hospitalized, tossed into the river, even killed dock workers and Communists until they cleared the waterfront. According to a British magazine, *Private Eye*, Brown paid out $225,000 for this and similar work in Italy and North Africa.

What is noteworthy about this is the fact that a *private* American organization should be so deeply involved in the *internal affairs* of foreign countries. Whenever the CIA is caught in such machinations there is a great hue and cry abroad as well as here at home. If it had been the U. S. Chamber of Commerce splitting unions, paying for intelligence activity, and organizing strikebreaking on foreign soil, public outcry would have reached a pitched crescendo. But the AFL-CIO leadership has been acting as a parallel, private CIA, for a quarter of a century, and as yet there have been no congressional investigations of its work.

Indeed, Meany and Lovestone became less inhibited with the passage of time. There was a hope after the merger of AFL and CIO in December 1955 that Walter Reuther would be able to drive Lovestone from the scene. But the hope proved vain, and collaboration with the government, instead of tapering off, has become more open.

Since 1961, three organizations have been formed to promote AFL-CIO work in Latin America, Africa, and Asia, paid for primarily out of AID funds.

The American Institute for Free Labor Development, the oldest and most ambitious, is unique in that it has sizable representation from management. Meany is its president, and Joseph Beirne its secretary-treasurer, but the board chairman is J. Peter Grace of W. R. Grace & Co., a firm which owns shipping companies, sugar haciendas, distilleries, box factories, textile mills, and what-have-you in Latin America.

Other officers include representatives of the Rockefeller interests, Anaconda Copper, Pan American Airways, all with large investments below the Rio Grande. Though the presence of these corporate titans in AIFLD is a distinct handicap in appealing to unionists, it was felt necessary to include them to slide the program through Congress. The two other groups, African-American Labor Center, headed by Brown, and the Asian-American Free Labor Institute headed by O'Keefe, avoided this difficulty by excluding employers.

The major activities of the three groups are education and social projects. Meany reported in August 1969 that 100,000 unionists in 20 Latin American countries have been through AIFLD's educational mill in their native surroundings, and 730 of the most promising were brought to the United States for extended studies at the Front Royal, Virginia institute.[7] The latter not only receive travel money and expenses while in the United States but are put on AIFLD's payroll for nine months after they return home. In British Guiana, as already noted, this period was extended a few months so that the graduates could devote their energies to the general strike aimed at toppling Jagan. For a favored few — about one tenth the number — there is an additional trip to Europe or Israel for further education.

Both the selection and the curriculum are designed to bring out the anti-communist strain. Here and there a leftist passes muster, but the overwhelming majority is recruited from moderate and right-of-center forces. A union research man in the U.S. who keeps close touch with AIFLD's work says that "all a Latin American has to do to get this bonanza is make a few strong anti-communist talks back home." The kind of people trained can be gauged from some of the resulting activity, as reported in AIFLD's bulletin: "Former AIFLD students help oust Reds from Uruguay Port Union"; "Two institute graduates challenge communist control of Honduran union." Student Hugo Solon Acero of the Confederation of Colombian Workers (CTC), we are told, eliminated "the last vestiges of communist influence in the regional federation of Cundinamarca." Another story reveals that George I. De Peana aided in the "ejection of [a] Red from presidency of a B.G. [British Guiana] union."

The curriculum, like the recruitment, is slanted in predictable directions. It is designed, as an AFL-CIO handout puts it, "to demonstrate that the pluralistic, democratic society has the best means of carrying forward the powerful changes sweeping through the southern half of the world — means which are vitally superior to those of totalitarianism." The listed classes at Front Royal, as of a couple of years ago, included, in addition to the usual ones on collective bargaining and grievance machinery, two sessions on the history of U.S. labor, two on the U.S. system of government, one on "totalitarianism," one on communism in Latin America, one on the politics of U.S. labor, one on the Sino-Soviet conflict, and one on the German labor movement. This heavy weight on subjects dear to the heart of the Meany-Lovestone team would seem to connote "indoctrination" more than "education," for it is quite obvious that the emphasis is on fashioning foreign unionists in the AFL-CIO image. It is difficult to see how classes in collective bargaining can be of any value, for instance, to unionists in Brazil where it doesn't exist. Even where true bargaining does exist, bread-and-butter unionism is not applicable to underdeveloped or developing countries where social change is the number one item on the historical agenda. The AFL-CIO leadership, however, seeks to transmit to other unionists abroad its own bias in favor of free enterprise, and against nationalization of industry, or government interference in business; and above all its bias in favor of permanent war against communism.

In addition to education the three institutes — AIFLD, AALC, and AAFLI — have social project departments. These have sponsored housing programs in 12 Latin American countries, including a large one in Mexico for the graphic trades unions with more than 3,000 units, as well as credit unions, some vocational training, and legal assistance. Again, unfortunately, the criteria for aid is based on the recipient union's impeccable record on communism. The design of the latter-day Lovestone program, like that of early postwar, is to build pockets of support within the lower classes for anti-communism and the Cold War.

The only significant difference is that the financing is now provided openly from the U.S. budget, rather than disguised. Ninety percent of the AIFLD, AALC, and AAFLI moneys are contributed by the Agency for International Development and spent around the world with little control by the embassies or the Government Accounting Office. The embassies in fact are instructed to hide the institutes' relationship with the U.S. government in order "to retain the union-to-union image."[8]

In effect, then, the $33 million spent on AIFLD, AALC, and AAFLI is not a "payoff," as Fulbright charges, but payment for services rendered the U.S. government which the government could not have performed itself. Whether a labor movement should be so closely identified with Washington, or whether Washington should tolerate this kind of open interference in the affairs of other nations, is another matter.

It is generally assumed by labor reporters that AIFLD, AALC, and AAFLI are used as recruiting grounds by the CIA for foreign agents. The list of students is available to CIA; it would be derelict in its duty if it didn't try to proselytize some of them.

In any event, there is an important parallel between what the Pentagon does with its counterinsurgency programs on the military front and what the AFL-CIO leadership does on the labor front. Both end up in the same place, and both speak the common language of the military-industrial complex. On at least two issues, anti-war dissent and foreign trade, the AFL-CIO brass is more strident than many conservative groups.

The AFL-CIO executive council in 1966, for instance, proclaimed that "while a minority has the right to dissent from the majority, disruption by even a well-meaning minority can only pollute and poison the bloodstream of our democracy. Those who would deny our military forces unstinting support are, in effect, aiding the communist enemy of our country . . ."[9]

On trade, an *AFL-CIO News* article of January 30, 1965 reports that at a Freedom Award dinner "George Meany challenged American free enterprise to refuse economic concessions to communist regimes whose basic aim is 'the destruction of democracy and the free enterprise system throughout the world.' "

Many of the groups that the labor hierarchy affiliates with are hard-line organizations which include the usual assortment of generals and businessmen associated with the military-industrial complex. The Citizens Committee for a Free Cuba — a right-wing anti-Castro force that lobbied for U. S. military conquest of Cuba — included in its roster of 44 prominent citizens Beirne; Brown; Lovestone; Paul Hall, president of the seafarers' union; Sal Hoffman, president of the upholsterers'; and Benjamin McLaurin, vice-president of the sleeping car porters'. Lovestone was at one time on the board of the American Security Council, the blacklist organization. He was also associated with the Council Against Communist Aggression, another right-wing group.

Militarism, it seems, draws many forces to its maw, including the major segment of America's labor leadership.

CHAPTER SEVEN

Academia in Harness

It is generally assumed that the most devastating war instrument known to man is the hydrogen bomb. But a secret briefing of congressmen by the Army early in 1969 revealed that the U.S. stockpile of nerve gas can kill the 3.4 billion people on earth many times over. One estimate given by an Army official was that there was enough to destroy no less than 100 billion people, 30 times the planet's population.[1]

Though President Nixon has partially curtailed the use of chemical and biological weapons (CBW), Associated Press reports that since 1960 the nation has spent $2.5 billion on awesome gases and germs; and that some 5,000 technicians and scientists are engaged in testing and developing poison chemicals ranging from the "mild" CS used in Vietnam to GA, GB, and V nerve agents that are odorless, tasteless, invisible, and can kill a human being in a matter of seconds. Some of these are stocked in Okinawa, West Germany, and one or two other places ready for immediate use.[2]

The potential killing power of biological agents is more difficult to estimate than that of chemical agents because the germs cannot be stored for more than a few days without becoming sterile. It is known, however, that the Pentagon keeps a strain of these deadly microbes alive at Pine Bluff, Arkansas, and in an emergency can reproduce them in large quantities at a few hours notice. What the capacity is and how many lives are threatened, is, of course, a military secret.

What is not secret — though our institutions of higher learning try zealously to hide it — is the role of our best universities in researching these frightening weapons. Without them CBW, like many other instruments of terror, could never have been developed to, what is euphemistically called, their present high level of "sophistication." The Army Chemical Center lists 11 universities collaborating on its poison gas program, including such prestigious schools as the UCLA Medical School, Baylor, Texas, Stanford Research Institute, Cornell Aeronautical Lab. The Army Biological labs list eight who experiment with death-dealing germs, including Johns Hopkins, Maryland, Minnesota, Yale, and the Illinois Institute of Technology. The Army Dugway Proving Ground, where a plane spraying nerve gas in 1968 missed its target and killed 6,000 sheep, has enlisted talent from IIT (Research Institute), Utah, Utah State, and the ever-present Stanford Research Institute, which is known as the "Pentagon of the West." The Air Force recruits brains for CBW from Cornell, IIT, and Florida; the Navy from the University of California at Berkeley.[3] Impressive as is this list it is incomplete: Seymour Hersh has published a Pentagon record of contractors in this field in 1967 that includes 52 colleges and universities, or one out of every 40 schools of higher learning in the country.[4]

The academic community's complicity in the development of gas-germ warfare is symptomatic of the broader marriage between academia and the military. It is part of that terrible drift toward Armageddon which drains away more and more energy from life-oriented pursuits to death-oriented ones, on the questionable theory that being prepared for mass killing will save us from mass death.

Before World War II academia stood on the sidelines of the military game. Weapons were not so complex that industry or the War Department had to call on the campus for help. Electronics were still rudimentary, nuclear physics still a preoccupation of the ivory towers with seemingly no practical value. The atom, it may be recalled, was split only in 1937, two years before hostilities broke out in Europe.

World War II, however, witnessed a qualitative change in weaponry, and with it a qualitative change in the relationship between the military and the professors. The Manhattan Project to develop the atom bomb, was the prototype of this relationship. At its height it enrolled thousands of scientists, most of whom were working on specialized subtasks without knowing what the final product would be. As nuclear energy research and electronics were harnessed to the war machine, considerable segments of academia were harnessed to the War Department.

The University of Chicago became the site of the first controlled chain reaction leading to the fabrication of an atom bomb. Massachusetts Institute of Technology (MIT) performed miracles in developing radar at its radiation laboratory. Johns Hopkins became the specialist in the self-deteriorating proximity fuse. The University of California did work on the atom bomb — and later the hydrogen bomb. Sonar, snorkels, guided missiles, walkie-talkies, jet planes, and many other weapons of war were the end result of basic and applied research on the campus. Equally important, the universities turned out the tens of thousands of scientists, engineers, and mathematicians to man the ramparts in factories, the War Department, and the new contract centers placed on many campuses.

When the war was over, academia had a choice of remaining conscripted to war research or breaking the umbilical cord. Some nationally-known scientists — like the late Leo Szilard — had second thoughts about the miracles they had wrought, especially with the atom bomb, and refused to go further. The wartime Office of Scientific Research and Development (OSRD) had been deactivated; there was dispute in professional ranks as to whether to go ahead with work on the hydrogen bomb. And the only agency making money available to the universities on a sizable scale was the Office of Naval Research.

Before long, however, the Pentagon realized the significance of research and development (R&D) for its future, and eager academics were ready again to accept its money. The Department of Defense's R&D budget has risen from a half billion a year at the end of the war to more than $8 billion; that of the

Atomic Energy Commission (AEC) from $37 million in 1947 to $1.7 billion in 1969; and the National Aeronautics and Space Administration (NASA) from $35 million to $4.6 billion. Of the $18 billion spent by the Government for this function (R&D) today, more than two thirds goes for these three agencies, and of these sums, something like $450 million annually is given to universities, and $700 million to university-related contract centers on which the universities are paid a management fee.[5]

If this sum seems small compared to what is allocated to industry for R&D, it should be noted that the 2,200 colleges and universities themselves spend only $10 billion a year for education. Key universities like MIT, Johns Hopkins, Stanford, and Maryland would be mammothly reduced in size and prestige if it were not for DOD, AEC, and NASA largesse.

MIT's R&D budget 1967-68, for instance, was $174 million, 95 percent of which came from federal government coffers, $120 million from defense sources alone. MIT, of course, is the ne plus ultra of academic collaboration with the military, but Michigan received $20 million in 1967 from these sources, Harvard $9 million, UCLA $13 million and the California network all told more than $70 million, Illinois $18 million, Yale $7 million, Columbia $18 million, Princeton $11 million.[6]

Most of these moneys go for *basic* and to some extent applied research, rather than development, so that they are far more important in the total scale of military procurement than the sums tend to indicate. It often costs hundreds of millions to develop a new weapons system whose utility was discovered in a university laboratory for a few hundred thousand of basic research.

The fact is, as former University of California president Clark Kerr has noted in his book *The Uses of the University*, that "intellect has also become an instrument of national purpose, a component part of the 'military-industrial complex.' "[7]

Air Force Secretary Robert C. Seamans, Jr., a former MIT professor and former deputy administrator of NASA, proclaims with all candor that "we cannot provide the necessary weapons for defense without the help of university research laboratories."[8]

The United States, he says, would suffer a severe technological setback if government-supported research were halted on the campuses.

John Hannah, president of Michigan State and a former Assistant Secretary of Defense, was even more forceful in 1961 when he insisted that "our colleges and universities must be regarded as bastions of our defense, as essential to the preservation of our country and our way of life as supersonic bombers, nuclear-powered submarines and intercontinental ballistic missiles."[9] Equating in importance the search for truth with supersonic bombers may disturb many of the half million professors and seven million students on campus, but there are more than a few who share Dr. Hannah's view.

"The era is one of war-in-peace," reads a 1957 explanation of why five leading universities teamed up to collaborate, through the Institute for Defense Analysis, with the Pentagon. It is an era in which vast shifts in the world power framework, aggravated by implacable communist ambitions of world domination, have brought us military responsibilities far beyond the direct defense of our country. . . . Such are the reasons why it is of paramount importance today not only to give all necessary support to weapons research, but also to the maintenance of the most effective possible bridge between military strategy and the total of technology — for converting technical advances into new elements of military power — for guiding technology in the creation of new and more effective foundations of strategy."[10]

This is a forthright defense of academia's links to the new militarism, worthy of the most sanguine general. The schools of higher learning, however, are, generally speaking, not so forthright; unlike other partners in the military-industrial complex, such as industry or the labor hierarchy, they approach their task with misgivings and grope for the ready rationale. For instance, the universities with CBW contracts "almost without exception . . . denied they were conducting such research" despite the fact that the Pentagon itself listed them as doing so. When Seymour Hersh queried them they gave one of three explanations:

1. The research was basic work and had no connection with CBW.
2. The research was unclassified work that was available to all.
3. The research was strictly defensive in nature.[11]

This has the familiar ring of George Meany's argument before Fulbright's committee that moneys used to buy satellite unions abroad were being spent only in the interests of "fraternal solidarity, humanitarianism in the best sense of the word."[12] The academic rationale is like the plea of the murderer that he was innocent because "I only pushed him out of the window, he fell 12 floors down all by himself." Admittedly not all Pentagon-paid research ends up in a weapon, and much of it has a practical use other than in weapons. But the Pentagon buys the research *in the hopes* it can be applied to weapons manufacture. Moreover, much of what is called defensive research has a startlingly direct use. Pennsylvania's Institute for Cooperative Research (ICR) claims that its work is defensive but among the studies conducted by Projects Summit and Spicerack in its laboratory after 1961 was secret research on defoliation and herbicides, soon to be used in Vietnam; and in its offices were ceiling-to-floor maps of Vietnam tagged, according to Hersh, "with brightly colored pins depicting various villages — or various targets. One protesting professor was told by an ICR worker that the institute received many calls from Vietnam, apparently linked to the defoliation program."[13] A subcontract by the institute with the Cornell Aeronautical Laboratory provided that the latter "conduct a detailed target analysis to determine anticipated target neutralization requirements."

On October 9, 1965 the director of Summit and Spicerack was quoted in the *Daily Pennsylvanian* as stating that his projects were developing aerial systems to disseminate arsenic compounds. Twenty days later Deputy Secretary of Defense, Cyrus Vance, admitted at a foreign policy conference that arsenic compounds were being used in Vietnam.[14] It stretches the imagination somewhat to call this kind of research defensive.

When guerrilla warfare in Vietnam began to mount after 1960, Cornell, Tulane, and Oklahoma universities were suddenly plied with contracts to inquire into incendiary weapons. Surveying the rugged terrain of Vietnam in many places, the Pentagon began thinking ahead to the future when "anti-personnel" arms, such as flamethrowers and napalm, might be needed to root out the insurgents. Tulane was engaged therefore to look into aspects of a "long-range portable flamethrower system," Oklahoma into the "susceptibility of potential target components to defeat by thermal action" — acadamese for how to kill guerrillas with incendiaries — and Cornell into such items as flame warfare, grenades, fire bombs, hydrocarbons, fuels, bomblets, white phosphorous, bomb clusters, incendiary gels (napalm).[15]

Schools like MIT or Johns Hopkins could not disguise their relationship to the military machine, even if they wanted to. But in many schools the administration either tries to downgrade its importance or explain it away. A Yale official, for instance, countered student charges that the school was engaged in CBW work, by insisting that the professor involved was doing a harmless study for the Army's CBW research center at Fort Detrick "in the epidemiological properties of viruses in the interest of a better understanding of the spread of certain diseases." It turned out, however, that one of the concerns of this particular academic was the artificial dissemination of the Eastern encephalitis virus which Brigadier General J. H. Rothschild lists in his book, *Tomorrow's Weapons*, as having "biological warfare interest."[16]

The University of Maryland medical school grudgingly accepted money from the Pentagon to study a certain type of disease on the rationale that it was research that fit into a *pattern* of nonmilitary studies it was doing. That was true, but the military obliged with the funds only because it relished hopes that the virus involved might make a good biological warfare agent.

The 54 professors who worked on the Michigan State University project in Vietnam from 1955 to 1960 knew that as a team they were acting as a "cover" for the U.S. government to violate the Geneva Accords. But many consoled themselves that individually they were doing worthwhile research in anthropology, economics, and other fields that was far removed from the activity of associates who did military and police training. Some of the research — such as a study of the Montagnards by Prof. Gerald C. Hickey or a survey of the economy by Prof. Frank C. Child — was of excellent quality.

Even those whose activity came closer to counterinsurgency

believed, as their final report put it, that they were "raising the general level of educational standards, and implanting in the minds of government officials, police officers and teachers the ideas of responsibility and responsiveness to the public . . . which is a prerequisite for the eventual evolution of free institutions in Vietnam."

Yet, the project was deliberately designed to circumvent an international agreement, to do what Washington itself could not do openly. Under those Accords, which the Eisenhower regime promised not to upset, foreign governments were prohibited from bringing to Vietnam "all types of arms" or to build up its military strength.

But Vice-president Richard Nixon himself visited President Hannah of MSU and asked him to undertake — under the guise of "advising" — the strengthening of Ngo Dinh Diem's forces. The main job of the MSU team was to train the palace guard (a virtual army), and the police, as well as to supply them with guns, ammunition, tear gas, trucks, grenades, and other weapons. According to Robert Scheer it also controlled the secret police.[17]

As a whole, this project was the most brazen interference by a university in the internal affairs of a foreign nation, and undoubtedly contributed to the full-scale war that later ensued under President Johnson. Individual professors, however, allayed their consciences by arguing that they were not involved in the "dirty work" part of the project.

The academic community's motives in doing war research are badly scrambled. "For some students," says an MIT professor, "there's a genuine aversion to defense-related work. But for others science is a cop-out, a way to avoid the draft." For still others there is the lure of a fast buck: "university technicians," a New Hampshire economist told the *Christian Science Monitor*, "are always asking if there isn't some defense contract around that they can work on to make extra money."[18]

Many are caught in a trap: their graduate work was in a field where few jobs are available other than defense-related ones. Since half of all R&D money today, according to *Look*, "is military in nature," it is easy to understand why so many young scientists are caught in its meshes. Forty-five percent of the MIT graduate students who sign up with industry accept jobs with the 100 large defense contractors.

Moreover, a large part of the money coming from DOD, AEC, and NASA is for basic research, rather than applied research or development. A physicist doing research at Argonne or Brookhaven is far removed from the practical work on hydrogen bombs that goes on at Livermore. His unclassified work is related to war only in the sense that he may discover a great new principle, like fission, that can later be turned into a military weapon. On the other hand, however, his discoveries can also bring mankind great civilian benefits. Even the man at Livermore may be assigned to basic research, and is related to war work only because he has agreed in advance to take on bomb research if asked to do so.

The same can be said of the space program. As of now, landing on the moon has no military significance; and scientists engaged in the moon-space project may feel no pangs of conscience about furthering the goals of militarism. But an integral part of the space program, little publicized, is the development of space stations which definitely have a military objective. Nuclear payloads can be mounted on them, free from any threat that the Russians or Chinese can intercept them. In the world of military research it is difficult to delineate where "peace" work ends and "war" work begins. Project Agile, for instance, is the Pentagon's major program for research in counterinsurgency, but one of its jobs a few years ago was to develop a new plastic container for the rice and "nucmon" sauce eaten by South Vietnamese soldiers. The scientists working on this subproject may have felt they were performing a nonwar service, but as *Newsweek* commented they were contributing "to raising the fighting potential of the Vietnamese G.I."[19]

Many scholars argue that science is "neutral"; the principles evolved, especially in basic research, can be applied for both war work and peace work. MIT's great complex, for instance, has applied what it has learned about guidance systems to the Apollo moon program, but was also responsible for convincing a skeptical DOD that it was feasible to develop a guidance system for the Poseidon (MIRV). Wherever one turns in the academic complex there is a similar duality: principles and projects have *both* civilian and military implications.

But whatever the motives of *individual* scholars or the means by which they assuage their conscience, there does exist an elite of universities and an elite of professors fully committed to the military-industrial complex. "Those who run the universities," writes James Ridgeway in his classic book on academia, *The Closed Corporations*, strive "to preserve . . . the myth of their independence from Government." But "there is little real interest . . . in altering their fundamental relationship with the Defense Department."[20]

Money corrupts, and big money corrupts grandiosely. Just as the 100 top defense contractors receive the bulk of Pentagon contracts, so the largest and most prestigious universities get the major share of DOD, AEC, and NASA money. There are sizable grants from the Department of Health, Education, and Welfare nowadays, but the largest portion is still defense-related. A congressional study in 1964 showed that 10 universities (out of 2,200 institutions of higher learning) receive 38 percent, and 50 receive three quarters of all federal funds given to colleges and universities for R&D. "Thus," says Ridgeway, "80 percent of MIT's funds are estimated to come from the Government [including nondefense sources]; Columbia and Princeton get about 50 percent of their money from Washington."[21] The California Institute of Technology, formerly headed by President Nixon's science advisor, Lee A. DuBridge, and now by former Air Force Secretary Harold Brown, was given $3.5 million by the Pentagon for research in 1968, and $5 million by NASA and AEC — much more than what it received from its whole student body in tuition.[22] In addition it received a management fee for running NASA's Jet Propulsion lab which has a $214 million a year budget.

Grand new buildings that might otherwise not be built on these prestigious campuses rise up only because of military funds. The Stanford Space Engineering and Science Building was erected with $2,082,000 from NASA and $992,000 from the Air Force. The materials science program begun a decade ago underwrote new facilities at Brown and Cornell, among others. And more important than the buildings are the computers and technical equipment which might also be out of the university's reach without Pentagon largesse.

The schools sometimes camouflage this materialist bent in idealistic phrases. A special faculty committee at Princeton in 1967 said that the school's tie with IDA "symbolizes a choice by the university to integrate itself into the life of the nation, to relate itself to the pressing problems of contemporary society, and to acknowledge its obligations to the defense of the society of which it is a part." But the Pentagon, speaking of its CBW research shortly before, was more direct in explaining the motives that have wedded academia to the military: "To perform this research in some cases requires expensive and complicated equipment . . . use of this research equipment is not restricted and performed solely for BW/CW use. Therefore, the material benefits which result to the universities are evidence from the equipment which is paid for by federal funding."[23]

Government money also draws to the top universities specializing in war work many of the best professors and the best students. A survey published by Brookings some years ago revealed that one quarter of the scientists at 12 top universities received part of their regular salaries from federal funds, and that at one of these schools there were 151 professors whose full pay came from federal coffers. To expect such men to be disinterested in government policy or militarism is stretching human nature a little too far.

A professor working at one of the federally funded research and development centers (contract centers) administered by such schools as Johns Hopkins, Columbia, MIT, or University of California is assured a salary much higher than he might get either as a teacher or working directly for the Pentagon. Thousands do consulting work for industry or think-tanks on the side, greatly augmenting or even doubling what they earn at the university or contract center. Academics from Yale, Princeton, Harvard, and Columbia earn up to $200 a day plus expenses consulting at the Institute for Defense Analysis (IDA).[24]

Parenthetically it might be noted that Harvard, which prides itself on refusing classified research (though it is not *entirely* true, as witness a project for the Army Chemical Corps in the early 1960s on "lethal and incapacitating agents research") nonetheless permits its professors to engage in classified projects off campus as consultants.[25] Indeed the contract centers and think-tanks utilize many professors as consultants or part-time employees, while permitting the universities to languish in the fiction that they themselves are independent of war work.

Many academics become rich in spin-off operations from research they first did for the military. Simulmatics Corporation, for instance, was established by a public relations man and three professors from MIT, Columbia, and Yale, to estimate "possible human behavior by the use of computer technology" — fields they researched at their schools, much of it with government money. Simulmatics now receives federal money to do secret research on such items as sampling opinion in Vietnam.

Along Route 128 in Massachusetts there are 160 such spin-off firms from MIT alone, and more from Harvard, where professors continue to do what they were doing at contract centers and continue to receive DOD money, but now pocket the profits as private entrepreneurs.[26] A similar complex of 200 aerospace and electronics firms exists around Stanford on the West Coast.[27]

J. Sterling Livingston, a professor at Harvard Business School, set up a half dozen such spin-off companies, one of them in partnership with Paul R. Ignatius (who later became Secretary of the Navy) to teach the Pentagon techniques in procurement and management. *Look* cites the case of William Rambo, a Stanford dean who is director of the Stanford electronics laboratories and a member of several Pentagon advisory committees, but also owns shares and is on the board of an electronics firm that holds $80 million in defense contracts.

Profits and higher earnings, of course, are not the only factors that drive the academic community into the military-industrial complex. There is also the matter of equipment and grants.

It takes hundreds of thousands of dollars — sometimes millions — to equip the modern physics or biology laboratories. For those who want to toe the militarist line, that money is available from the three militarist sources. A professor or graduate student who wants the best facilities to work with is virtually forced toward these institutions. That is where he can do the most advanced work, and that is where the prestige is. This is not only true in the physical sciences, but in behavioral ones that are so dependent these days on expensive computers.

Some years ago Prof. Kenneth Boulding of Michigan tried to get $250,000 for his Center for Research and Conflict Resolution to study unilateral initiatives that might mitigate the arms race. He was turned down cold by DOD. Boulding had to subsist on a $30,000 a year budget raised by the school and from private sources.

On the other hand, the Center for Research in Social Sciences (CRESS) and the Human Resources Research Office (HumRRO), which do work for the Army, have received many millions for social science studies. CRESS, part of the American University complex at Washington, handled — under a different name — Project Camelot which studied counterinsurgency problems in Chile and many other places. HumRRO, at George Washington University, trains soldiers in firing anything from an M-1 rifle to a Nike Zeus missile and gives them quick language courses and other skills needed for counterinsurgency.[28]

The stench from these activities has led both schools to begin severing ties with the contract centers, but their work will continue independently and the Army will probably continue to pick up the tab — though perhaps in reduced amounts. If Professor Boulding was unable to get money for peace research, there is plenty around for seminars on student violence held in Puerto Rico and funded by the Air Force. The sociologists in this instance were much less critical of militarism than Boulding.

Far too many professors and schools let themselves be drawn to "where the money is." They outline projects for DOD and its two associates, AEC and NASA, not necessarily because that is their main scholarly interest but because that is where the money can be procured. Their research becomes *mission* research for a government agency, rather than the quest for knowledge based on their own proclivities. In the course of time, therefore, there has emerged a solid complex of civilian militarists on the campus who foster and promote mission research. These are the professors who serve on a host of government advisory boards, such as the Defense Science Board (DSB), the President's Science Advisory Committee (PSAC), the Air Force Science Advisory Board (AFSAB), and those of the other services.[29]

From the University of California alone there are 18 such professors, including Edward Teller. From Princeton there are nine, from Stanford eight. Even a Nobel prize winner gets sucked in on occasion. James D. Watson, one such laureate, served on the President's chemical and biological warfare advisory panel from 1961 to 1964. These are all men who are deeply involved in funneling research money to the campus, and thereby keeping the campus oriented toward the military-industrial complex.

As with other segments of the complex there is also considerable shuttling back and forth between government and academia (as well as industry). It is no accident, for instance, that the three men who have held the post of director of defense research and engineering at DOD, including the present one, John S. Foster, Jr., came from the Livermore big bomb laboratory. The president of the University of California which operates Livermore and Los Alamos, among many other defense projects, is Charles Hitch, former Assistant Secretary of Defense. The vice-president of the University of Rochester, which has increased defense contracts from $1 million to $13 million in two years, is Robert L. Sproull, chairman of the Defense Science Board. Dr. James R. Killian, Jr., chairman of the MIT corporation, was the country's first presidential science advisor.[30] In addition university officials are heavily represented on the boards of large corporations with a considerable interest in defense contracts. James R. Killian, Jr., chairman of the corporation at MIT, is on the board of General Motors; Franklin D. Murphy, chancellor at the University of California, on the board of Ford; Edwin D. Harrison, president of the Georgia Institute of Technology, and Frederick L. Hovde, president of Purdue, on General Electric; George E.

Pake, provost of Washington University, on McDonnell; Dr.
Willard F. Libby, director of the Institute of Geophysics and
Planetary Physics at UCLA, on Douglas Aircraft; William A. M.
Burden, of Columbia, is a director of Lockheed, and is associated
with IDA and the Farfeld Foundation which channeled a million
dollars of CIA money to the Congress for Cultural Freedom.[31]
Men such as these have institutionalized the military-industrial-
academic relationship into a pivotal part of American militarism.

What this does to academia itself is a subject of much debate.
But there is no question that, as with everything else about the
military-industrial complex, it has greatly distorted campus
priorities. It has placed a premium on research as against teaching. It has strengthened the larger and most prestigious schools
as against the smaller ones. A couple of years ago the Pentagon
tried to ameliorate this situation somewhat by initiating Project
Themis to channel research money to smaller schools, but it is
allocated only $27 million a year and has been far from a success.

Though the amount of secret work on campus proper has been
reduced in the past year (by about $10 or $12 million), secrecy is
still an invidious part of defense-sponsored research especially
in the contract centers where hundreds of millions are annually
spent on classified work. Secrecy not only runs alien to academic
tradition which requires research to be publishable, but it creates
a body of professors who seem to be afraid to speak out on vital
issues.

A high official of an eastern university told two *Chicago Daily
News* reporters, when asked to comment on the military-industrial complex: "I must be careful of what I say. I have millions in research I'm in charge of. Now that's off the record."[32]

During the one-day protest by scientists against war research
March 4, 1969, Dr. Greg Dunkel of the University of Maryland's
physics department noted that "every theoretical physicist" had
signed petitions for the day of protest, "but the 'experimentalists'
didn't. You see, all the theoretician needs is money for his salary
and a generous supply of pencils and paper, but the experi-
mentalist needs fantastically complex equipment. I know one,
for instance, who had a $100,000 budget for his Ph.D. thesis.
That's why the experimentalists won't buck the military."

Most of all, the military-academic complex, as already noted, has diverted energies from life-enriching research to death-oriented work. It is hardly a coincidence that four times as much money was spent on CBW research as on studies to relieve cancer.[33]

Student militants may demonstrate ceaselessly against Dow Chemical for producing napalm to bomb the people of Vietnam, but napalm was not developed by Dow. It was invented at Harvard by a Harvard professor.

Innumerable scientific ventures become corrupted or distorted by real or fancied military needs. The universities of Miami, California, Columbia, Oregon, Washington, and Hawaii are currently helping the Navy with an oceanography project. The oceans, as everyone knows, are future storehouses of food and precious minerals. But as Seymour Hersh points out in a *Ramparts* article, the Navy has different ideas. Its long-term planning includes "deep-running, quiet submarines (that) will circulate near the ocean floor, 6,000 feet below the surface, each one capable of hurling megaton-force missiles at targets more than 5,000 miles away. Underwater cities with depots and nuclear recharging facilities will service these vessels" as well as provide undersea shelters for rest and recreation.[34]

Back in 1961 President Eisenhower warned that "the prospect of domination of the nation's scholars by federal employment, project allocations, and the power of money is ever present."

Nobel prize professor George Wald, speaking on Pentagon and armament influence in his much heralded speech March 4, 1969, said it more forcefully: The Pentagon "is corrupting the life of the whole country. It's bought up everything in sight; it's even bought up the labor unions. It's made astonishing inroads into science. . . ."

CHAPTER EIGHT

An Alternative to Catastrophe

Challenges to the military-industrial complex, like those of Dr. Wald, have increased in cadence with the realization that the Pentagon has failed in Vietnam. Perhaps that is one of the dominoes that militarists have said would fall if America did not win in Southeast Asia. In any case, counterforces are emerging to challenge the complex. Students are demanding that their schools sever ties with the Pentagon and related agencies. Liberal organizations are holding conferences on "national priorities." Senators and congressmen are probing military spending as never before. And the radical youth have escalated their opposition to the Vietnam War into opposition to the war machine per se.

The debate on the military-industrial complex has begun, and on its outcome may depend not only the survival of the United States but the whole of humanity. It is certainly of greater urgency than the debate over the French Revolution in the 1790s, over slavery from 1830 to 1865, or over the depression of 1929. When the dust clears, the debate will hinge on a single question: Are the assumptions on which the military-industrial complex were created valid, partly valid, or totally false? Proponents of the first position — that the assumptions are valid — will urge economy in spending; proponents of the second position, that the military be "controlled" so that the nation can restructure its "priorities"; and proponents of the third position, that the complex is fighting the wrong war, at the wrong time, with the wrong weapons and must be entirely eliminated.

The argument that the Pentagon is wasteful and inefficient is an attractive one to large numbers of people who are worried about taxes and inflation. "It is responsibly asserted," editorializes the *Wall Street Journal*, "that $10 billion or more a year could be cut from the military budget without impairing national security."[1] If the $10 billion could be chipped away, the economy would be healthier, the burdens on the American people lighter. This thesis may or may not be true (a cut in federal spending can *also* lead to unemployment), but it does not come to grips with more fundamental issues: Are the purposes for which the complex was created justified? Can we avoid a "garrison state" so long as it continues to exist?

To assuage economy critics, Defense Secretary Laird announced in late August 1969, a reduction in the proposed defense budget of $3 billion a year. One hundred thousand men, he pledged, would be cut from the 3.4 million military forces by June 1970, and 100 ships retired from the Navy. He coupled his promise with the warning that he was doing it only "under congressional pressure" and that any further gymnastics with the budget would be "a very dangerous course."[2] To emphasize the point, Laird hinted at a new Russian threat, namely that "the Soviet Navy has more ships deployed away from the Soviet Union than ever before."

This is, as James Reston of *The New York Times* suggests, a time-honored game:

First, some military spokesman declassifies intelligence information about the rise of Soviet naval power. Next some admiral makes a speech about the decline of America's control of the seas. And finally, the Secretary of Defense announces some cuts in the defense budget, but warns that more cuts will damage the nation's capacity to keep the peace.[3]

Transparent or not, the technique seems to work moderately well. It certainly was a contributing factor to the defeat of the Senate liberals who in the summer of 1969 tried for 38 days to whittle the $20 billion authorization bill. All they could show for their effort was a slash of $71 million, mostly from Pentagon social research.

Although Americans talk endlessly about the need to eliminate "waste" and "inefficiency" from the federal budget, the argument about *military* waste and *military* inefficiency evidently leaves them lethargic. A decade ago Senator Proxmire's close friend, former Illinois Senator Paul Douglas, engaged in a similar campaign against Pentagonian waste and recited similar factors about excessive costs brought to light by the General Accounting Office. Based on these revelations Jules Duscha of the *Washington Post* wrote an article listing instance after instance of multimillion overcharges by Lockheed, Western Electric, and other industrial titans.[4] Articles and books on the subject appeared in copious numbers, but the critics could not overcome the counterargument that such excesses were of minor importance in face of the desperate need for a strong military establishment.

Secretary Laird repeats this defiance of the critics today: Do they deny, he wants to know, "the facts of international life that make necessary the maintenance of a strong military force by the United States? Do they believe that such a force can be equipped by the village blacksmith producing weapons in his spare time?" Laird admits there are certain practices that need changing, such as the deliberately low bids made by defense contractors who know that costs will run much higher. But he insists that the military-industrial complex "has provided the tools of national defense . . . with an efficiency that is not approached in any other nation of the world."[5] If one accepts the need for a strong military establishment, arguments about waste seem like nit-picking — like a man disputing a surgeon's bill in a heart transplant.

Liberals, in and out of Congress, couple their charge of waste with one about distorting national priorities. The problem, as Senator Proxmire sees it, is "how can we balance our military needs and expenditures with our domestic problems and needs?"[6] He accepts the thesis that we need *both* guns and butter, but holds that we are spending too much on one and too little on the other. What the nation requires, as the liberals see it, is not only to curtail waste and arrest inflation, but to meet pressing welfare demands for the underprivileged. A report of congressional dissidents who met privately in June 1969 argued, therefore, that "if we are to increase substantially our expenditures on domestic needs, we must correspondingly reduce our expenditures on the military." Priorities can be reversed, they said, if Congress were to secure the necessary information to rebut the military and make a concerted campaign to win public support. They propose the formation of a Defense Review Office which would dig out defense information and analyze its significance for the legislators, and a Temporary National Security Committee, made up of congressmen, senators, and private citizens, to "conduct a critical examination . . . of the military-industrial establishment."[7]

John Kenneth Galbraith, statesman, professor, and former national chairman of Americans for Democratic Action, speaks in the same vein. The cover of his recent book, *How to Control the Military*, carries the modest blurb that "when the Vietnam War ends, $6 to $7 billion could be freed to save our cities, feed the hungry, give all Americans a chance at a decent life." One may question whether $7 billion can do — or begin to do — all these wonderful things, but the liberals have concluded that by "controlling" the Pentagon they can redirect money from military coffers to useful social projects. The statement by Daniel P. Moynihan, President Nixon's special advisor for urban affairs, that programs already on the books "are going to eat up any revenue produced by the war's end," had not dissuaded them.

One way to effect the necessary controls, Galbraith suggests, would be through "a special body of highly qualified scientists and citizens to be called, perhaps, the Military Audit Commission." Its task would be "to advise the Congress and inform the public on military programs and negotiations."[8] Congressman Robert L. Leggett of California proposes that the military can be curbed by allocating to it a specific share of the federal budget — "say 50 percent or 60 percent." Prof. Richard A. Falk, former consultant to the Senate Foreign Relations Committee, feels the figure can be trimmed to "between 10 and 25 percent of the present level," in other words to something between $8 and $20 billion a year, if the Pentagon is forced to assess realistically "the kinds of threats that confront the United States." Instead of "working for weapons breakthroughs," says Falk, "and designing against unlikely contingencies, we need to work for a stabilized arms environment sustained at a minimum cost and risk."[9]

Implicit in the liberal critique is the notion that America *does* need a military establishment for defense, but it does not need one so large that it creates in its wake a self-propelling military-industrial bureaucracy which whittles away the power of Congress and the people. John Foster Dulles, oddly enough, made much the same point a long time ago, in a January 2, 1949 interview with *U.S. News & World Report:*

> I am inclined to think that we are exaggerating the percentage of our national income that needs to be diverted into military establishment. I think that there is, as I say, a risk of war, but I think the risk is not so great that we should seriously jeopardize our own economic health as a free society by saddling ourselves with such vast armament.

History shows, unfortunately, that the military spigot can be turned on much easier than it can be turned off. If a nation is ready to accept the simple theorems on which militarism is predicated — whether real or made to look real — each crisis will evoke the demand for "more." The "communist menace" conjured up after World War II made it possible to increase the peacetime military budget from prewar levels of a billion or less to $12 billion and $14 billion in the first postwar years. The Korean crisis of 1950 prompted Congress to give DOD authority to raise spending from $14.5 billion to $53.5 billion in a single year. Actual expenditures doubled from 1951 to 1952, from $20.7 billion to $41.3 billion. The Vietnam crisis in 1965 catapulted the Pentagon's spending from $50 billion a year to $80 billion four years later. If that budget is now slashed by $3 billion or the $7 to $10 billion that *realpolitik* liberals are urging, the *power* of the military-industrial complex will be affected only slightly. And its spokesmen and theoreticians will soon be scurrying for new "crises" on which to peg their argument for more preparedness.

In a world consumed by revolution and power struggles, crises crop up as frequently as the full moon. We must expect, says Prof. C. E. Black in his *Dynamics of Modernization,* "10 to 15 revolutions a year for the foreseeable future in the less developed societies."[10] Each of these revolutions alters the international balance of power to some degree; each can break out into the kind of civil war which resulted in intervention in Vietnam. Henry A. Kissinger, White House national security advisor, has asked the Rand Corporation, according to Flora Lewis, to conduct studies on such subjects as "the danger and extent of insurgency in Thailand," "circumstances in which the government of Brazil might be overthrown if it decides to expropriate U.S. assets," and "circumstances in which U.S. nuclear weapons might be used in the Middle East."[11] Obviously each of these is a crisis area which occupies the thoughts of President Nixon's key foreign policy aide, and under certain circumstances can be manufactured into a synthetic war scare.

A new type of guerrilla movement is developing in Latin America — the *city* guerrilla — called "Tupamaros" in Uruguay and "Marighellistas" in Brazil. If they achieve their objective of overthrowing their governments, will that trigger a demand for accelerated military spending — to thwart the "Fidelista menace?" The "Nasserist" government in Peru, in addition to nationalizing some American property, has been seizing American fishing vessels less than 200 miles offshore; any one of these seizures can result in killings and a consequent call by militarists here for action. The six-day war of June 1967 in the Middle East has turned into a continuing war, with both great powers heavily involved on opposite sides. Should the Israelis accidentally bomb a Soviet ship in Egyptian waters and the Soviets retaliate, the military faction here would certainly try to pyramid this into a crisis demanding more defense spending. In Laos, according to Senate Majority leader Mike Mansfield, American troops are doing some actual fighting on the side of the Souvanna Phouma government and have taken some casualties.[12] The communist-oriented Pathet Lao has made considerable progress until recently, and there is a faction in the government ranks friendly to the communist side that is reported ready to take power. Should that happen there would undoubtedly be a cry in the United States for intervention. Each of these is a crisis area that can explode with little warning and give the American military-industrial complex its opportunity to fan the flames for more preparedness. Or, it could be the seizure of American oil interests by the new revolutionary government of Libya. Or another *Pueblo* incident near North Korea. Or a guerrilla attack against Seoul, South Korea. Or a Soviet foray into Romania. The possibilities are endless.

Those possibilities are inherent in the purpose of the military-industrial complex. The complex is not a popular force with disinterested goals. It is, instead, a conglomerate of elites — a military elite, an industrial elite, a banking elite, a labor elite, an academic elite — which seeks its own aggrandizement through global expansion. It has sponsored for that purpose what Hanson Baldwin calls "a surge of nationalism," the concept that "America ought to rule the world." Harry Truman defined it more specifically as assuring the dominance of free enterprise economies over regimented ones. In economic terms that means enlarging American trade and investment, as well as finding new sources of raw materials. In political terms it means aiding those regimes favorable to America's economic goals. In military terms it means nuclear deterrence (or damage-limitation) to checkmate the only power capable of stymieing those ambitions, the Soviet Union. It translates itself inevitably into military bases around the world, military pacts, contingency agreements, and actual intervention where necessary and feasible, to help friendly regimes that are tottering or friendly forces that aspire to power against neutralists and Communists. The power elite that is now called the military-industrial complex has, in other words, fashioned a blueprint for "Pax Americana" that would do for the twentieth century what "Pax Britannica" did for the nineteenth. It would create the international setting in which American private interests could advance unchecked. British historian, Arnold J.

Toynbee, by no means anti-American or pro-Communist, describes America's present role as "leader of the worldwide anti-revolutionary movement in defense of vested interests."[13]

It is no accident that Washington has been almost universally on the side of conservative forces in the developing areas — Syngman Rhee in Korea, Chiang Kai-shek in China, the Shah in Iran, the militarists throughout Latin America, the king in Jordan, the king in Saudi Arabia, the military regimes in Thailand, Laos, and Vietnam. These conservative elements, to secure their own "vested interests," have been willing to accept American military and economic support in return for concessions to American "vested interests." Nor is it an accident that by and large the same legislators — Stennis, Russell, Rivers, Mundt, Goldwater, Tower, McClellan, to name a few — who are the fiercest advocates of military spending and military ventures, are also the fiercest opponents of social programs such as medicare, higher minimum wages, antipoverty, social security, and favorable trade union legislation.

Put crassly, the military-industrial complex has defined America's goal as being the bastion of the status-quo — abroad and at home. Given that national purpose it is folly to expect any *enduring controls* over the military establishment or the complex it fosters. If we believe in taxes we must have tax collectors, and if we believe in global expansion we must have a military-industrial complex. The restructuring of national priorities can only proceed with a repudiation of the complex's definition of national purpose and a re-education of the citizenry as to its folly.

The American people of course are not the authors of the expansionist policy and whatever they have gained from it is ephemeral and illusory. But they have been mobilized behind it by a combination of fear and pride — fear that the Communists, as General Curtis E. LeMay puts it, seek "control of the entire world" including the United States, and pride that military power has made us strong. For a quarter of a century Americans have believed these conventional wisdoms: communism was the implacable enemy, the Pentagon our primary defense against it.

America had won World War II through military-industrial power; this was a good enough formula against a new enemy.

But the predigested clichés which have won the people to the Pentagon are in fact dangerous half-truths which, if not repudiated, augur catastrophe. History proves that a nation that prepares for the wrong war has little chance of avoiding defeat. France, for instance, believed that its Maginot Line would protect it from Germany just as its trenches had done in the World War I "war of position." It found to its dismay that the German *blitzkrieg* — war of movement — had upset all the old strategies. Is it possible that the United States too has been preparing for the wrong war against the wrong enemy?

Conceding the dictatorial character of Soviet communism and the crimes it has committed — in Hungary and Czechoslovakia, for instance — it must be clear in sober reflection that communism is not now and never has been the *cause* of world disturbances, but the *effect* of them. It is not THE enemy, but a DERIVATIVE of the true enemy — hunger, disease, illiteracy, poverty, and war. George F. Kennan points out that communism would not have entrenched itself even in the Soviet Union if the West had not insisted that Kerensky's liberal government in 1917 continue the war and postpone reforms.[14] Lenin and Trotsky rode to power, though their party was only a minority to begin with, on the tide of three words — peace, bread, land.

Subsequently the West tried to do in the Soviet Union what the United States is now doing in Vietnam. For two and a half years, from spring 1918 to autumn 1920, 14 foreign armies occupied Soviet territory and hundreds of millions of dollars were given by Britain and France to former Czarist officers seeking to topple the Red regime. Japan alone sent 72,000 soldiers to Siberia. According to Stephen Pichon, French foreign minister, there were in March 1919, 850,000 allied troops in South Russia alone — French, British, Romanian, Italian, Serb, and Greek. The purpose of this effort, as Winston Churchill, then Secretary of War in the British cabinet, stated it, was to strangle "the baby in its crib."

But Churchill in 1920, like American leaders today, failed to understand the inner vitality of a revolution. Russia was then a military cipher — 76 percent of its troops were dead, wounded, prisoners, or deserters — but Trotsky, by appealing to the patriotism of former Czarist officers, was able to enlist 30,000 to forge a modest Red army. Simultaneously Lenin appealed to the peasants by giving them land — while "our side," Generals Kolchak and Deniken (yesterday's Generals Thieu and Ky) took land *from* the peasants and gave it *back* to the landlords. Before long the peasants, lukewarm at first, were entirely with the Bolsheviks and their guerrilla forces were harassing the White Guards on every front. "The rapid collapse" of the conservative grouping, wrote Walter Duranty of *The New York Times*, "was greatly aided by guerrilla activities behind their front lines in which middle peasants and artisans took a vigorous part."[15]

The Soviet leaders also played skillfully on the desire of tired allied soldiers to go home. "Comrades," they said in leaflets and other forms of propaganda, "why are you fighting us? We don't want to fight. We want to be let alone. You go home and we'll go home." American troops sang "home toot sweet" and staged a near-mutiny to force their withdrawal. A serious mutiny in Odessa by the French fleet caused France to evacuate that city. All over Europe and America there were demonstrations by liberals, churchmen, mild socialists, and the newly-established communist movements for "hands off Russia." Longshoremen and sailors refused to load or man ships carrying munitions for the enemies of the Soviets. The intervention failed.

Kennan writes:

Never, surely, have countries contrived to show themselves so much at their worst as did the allies in Russia from 1917 to 1920. Among other things, their efforts served everywhere to compromise the enemies of the Bolsheviki and to strengthen the Communists themselves. So important was this factor that I think it may well be questioned whether Bolshevism would ever have prevailed throughout Russia had the Western governments not aided its progress to power by this ill-conceived interference.[16]

Anti-communism had strengthened, not weakened, communism.

The lessons of 1918-20 have never been digested in the West

and certainly not by the military-industrial complex in the United States. The pattern of supporting conservatives and militarists against national revolutions in the name of "fighting communism," has indeed been enshrined as high policy.

Communism sank roots in China in much the same way as in the Soviet Union, capitalizing on a similar refusal by the West to deal with social problems and a similar intoxication with the military response. The Chinese revolution, we tend to forget, did not begin in 1949 when the Communists seized power, but in 1911 — six years *before* the world had heard anything about Bolshevism or communism. It was led by a physician named Sun Yat-sen, and directed against the foreign powers which had seized China's land, operated its ports, imposed extra-territorial rights, and had done everything to keep China disunited and impotent, as well as against the native Manchu Dynasty. Sun quickly disposed of the Manchu but he was unable immediately to unify the country, evict the foreigners, or convert the feudal land system. For 15 years the Chinese revolution not only had to contend with the many war lords who contained it in the southern part of the country, but the world powers who subsidized these warlords. But if the West would not heed the cry of nationalism, Moscow was more than willing — and the Chinese had no other place to go. Sun Yat-sen's Kuomintang made an agreement with the Soviets and invited communist technicians and advisors to build a revolutionary army, organize unions, peasant movements, and para-military units. With this aid Sun and his brother-in-law, Chiang Kai-shek, evicted the warlords and did unify the country.

In the process, however, after Sun had died, Chiang broke with the Communists and executed thousands in a terrible bloodbath. The West had an opportunity even then to pressure Chiang for major reforms, to make nationalism meaningful instead of stagnant and conservative. But it did none of these things. In these circumstances many nationalists turned to the Communists — as they were to do a few years later in Indochina. The noncommunist Fourth Army deserted to Mao Tse-tung and became the nucleus of the communist army. Tens of thousands of

Kuomintang members, literati, professors, members of the middle class, and socialists — including Sun's wife — joined with the Communists to complete Sun Yat-sen's dream of nationalism. While Chiang and his friends were enriching themselves, seizing hundreds of thousands of acres of land for their private use, the Communists were dividing the land among the common peasants. This was the bridge to power. As D. F. Fleming observes: "The peasant revolution was in the womb of history. In refusing to midwife its birth the Kuomintang left the opportunity by default to the Communists. . . . When the time came that the unfinished revolution could no longer be stopped, the Kuomintang had to be swept away and logically, the Communists had to win."[17]

The myth has evolved in recent years that the Communists could have been vanquished if only we had given more weapons to Chiang Kai-shek, or if we had sent American troops into the fray. Neither of these claims has merit. Chiang controlled the major cities of China and at least three quarters of the population when his regime began to totter. His government received $3 billion in aid from the United States, plus weapons from a million disarmed Japanese soldiers. It had four million men under arms and mountains of American hardware. Former Secretary of State Dean Acheson said:

> Nobody, I think, says that the nationalist government fell because it was confronted by overwhelming military force which it could not resist. . . . What has happened in my judgment is that the almost inexhaustible patience of the Chinese people in their misery ended. . . . The Communists did not create this condition. . . . But they were shrewd and cunning enough to mount it, to ride this thing into victory and into power.[18]

Foster Hailey, a former *New York Times* correspondent confirms this estimate:

> The reason the Communists finally won China was because they based their campaign on the people, the great, inert mass of 500,000,-000 from which Chiang and his inner circle had held themselves as remote since 1928 as does the Dai Lama from Western civilization. The Communists put their hopes in the political activation of the illiterate peasant and the underprivileged worker by promising him a

change. Chiang put his hopes in a military campaign, financed by the United States, that would maintain the status quo. It was in-evitable that in the long run the Communists would win.[19]

Where communism has achieved its glory it has not done so because of its military strength or its superior insights into dialectical materialism or the theory of surplus value, but because it gave leadership to men in misery whose plight the West and its native allies refused to ameliorate. This story was to be repeated in Cuba, Indochina, Algeria, and elsewhere. The mil-itary-minded in the United States like to argue that Castro was successful in Cuba because Washington cut off the shipment of arms to Fulgencio Batista. But Batista had at his disposal an army of 43,000 men, trained and supplied by the United States until almost the end; while Castro began with 80-odd men, decimated quickly to a dozen, and never numbering more than 1,200 guerrillas. It was not military force that plummeted him to power, but social force. The Cuban people were tired of a regime that was killing its opponents, that embezzled hundreds of millions of dollars, that tolerated unemployment of one third the work force. Castro won because of the social ills of his country. Three quarters of the sugar workers labored only three or four months a year, during the *zafra* (harvest) season. More than a third of the population was totally illiterate, another third partially so. In the farm sections, 90 percent of the people suf-fered from worm diseases, such as dysentery, or from anemia. Only 9 percent of the rural homes had electricity, 2 percent inside piping for water, and 3 percent indoor toilets. While American Ambassador Arthur Gardner looked upon Batista as Uncle Sam's "best friend," the lower classes of Cuba looked to Castro for liberation.

If these illustrations prove anything they prove that com-munism threatens the West only in the sense that Western fail-ures to alleviate social misery in the Third World have driven the native peoples toward revolution; and that the revolu-tionaries have turned, more frequently than not, to the Soviet Union and China for aid — on the theory that "the enemy of my enemy is my friend."

It is true that communism hopes to spread its wings worldwide — as does capitalism. Every nation, small or big, wants to enlarge its sphere of influence; it is in fact *inherent* in the very concept of *nationhood*. But the point is irrelevant.

Except for Eastern Europe, which was assigned to the Soviet sphere at the Yalta Conference, communism has not gained its victories by guns but by attaching itself to the postwar national revolution. That was certainly true in China, Indochina, and Cuba. And since those revolutions show remarkable resistance to being suppressed either by the guns of foreigners or by those of native dictators, the answer to communism obviously does not lie in military power.

A century ago England could conquer India with 50,000 troops. But in Algeria in recent years, France commanded 500,000 soldiers against 45,000 Algerian guerrillas, spent $3 million a day, $1 billion a year for seven and a half years, but was unable to subdue an infinitely weaker force. In Vietnam the United States and its allies command 1.5 million troops and spend $30 billion a year, but cannot defeat a vastly inferior force of 250,000 Vietnamese spending only a tiny fraction of what Washington does.

The salient characteristic of the last half of the twentieth century is that military power does not avail against social — revolutionary — power. Guns have certainly won a few victories for the United States — in Iran, Guatemala, Greece. Neutralism and communism have suffered setbacks in places like Indonesia and Brazil. And American military might was able to achieve stalemates in Berlin and Korea. But the tide of history is definitely running against militarism. All the "victories" for Western policies put together cannot compensate for the defection of China, with one fourth the world's population, from the Western orbit.

In a world that is in revolution — socially and technologically — military power actually makes the United States weaker. To assure bases and military agreements, the United States is forced into pacts with tyrants who reject social change. As each of these tyrants falls, America finds itself with fewer friends and greater problems. Chiang Kai-shek is replaced by Mao Tse-tung, Batista by Castro, Farouk by Naguib and Nasser, Nuri Said in Iraq by neutralist Kassem, Belaunde in Peru by the "Nasserist" Velasco Alvarado. The trend is inexorable.

After the war Albert Einstein observed that "the unleashed power of the atom has changed everything except our way of thinking. Thus we are drifting toward a catastrophe beyond conception."[20] The atom bomb beguiled Americans into believing that military power was their shield, when in fact military power no longer effectively serves political strategy. For the first time in history it is impossible to win a total war, and it is increasingly difficult even for great powers to win limited small ones.

This is a change of fundamental significance, the most important change in all civilized history. During the Punic wars Rome totally destroyed Carthage but civilization continued elsewhere. Now it is predestined that both a modern Rome and a modern Carthage will be simultaneously destroyed in nuclear war — it would be as General MacArthur said "double suicide."

Herman Kahn disputes this theory. He wrote some time ago:

Many believe that if one single button is pressed all the buttons will be pressed, and that some 30 minutes or so later, missiles will rain enough destruction to terminate the defender's existence as a nation; subsequently, some minutes or hours later, a similar rain of death and destruction will annihilate the attacking nation.

He wrote this in 1962 when, as he claimed, "missile forces are still small and limited, and the main striking power in both countries still lies in their bombers . . ."[21]

When missiles did indeed become intercontinental, Kahn elaborated a scenario of steps-to-escalation in which each power would show restraint — say by destroying a single city, then stopping. Now he is working on a scenario of damage limitation in which America would suffer "only" a few tens of millions dead while Russia lost its total population.

This may be attractive gamesmanship (fantasy?) for generals and civilian militarists. But it leaves out of account, assuming the nuclear game could be played this way, other weapons such as nerve gas, and more importantly the political results of a war in which 40 to 80 million Americans died.

How could a revolution be prevented *within* the United States under such frightful circumstances? And if a revolution were smashed, it could only be by a dictatorial military regime, so that the very thing we would be fighting against — totalitarianism — would come to pass through victory.

And what of the ambitions of other powers in the face of a decimated America? Would Mexico retake Texas and California; Canada bite off a slice of northern United States?

The escalation of technology has made militarism an anachronism; it cannot achieve victory in total war, it cannot effectively threaten small nations engaged in revolution — assuming this were desirable. What then remains?

Visionary as it may sound, our planet drifts toward the uncomfortable choice between one-world and no-world. Being "thy brother's keeper" has become a new law the great powers must heed, since they can no longer *conquer* other nations; they must *win* them to their side. Put differently, for the first time in history, it is not possible to be "practical" without being "moral."

President John F. Kennedy caught a glimmer of this truism in his first inaugural address when he told "those people in the huts and villages of half the globe struggling to break the bonds of mass misery" that "if a free society cannot help the many who are poor, it cannot save the few who are rich."[22] If the "strong" societies do not help the "revolution of rising expectations" in the weak ones, they face endless chaos and war until they themselves are destroyed.

The two billion people in the world who go to bed hungry every night, and live on $1 or $2 a week, will accept only radical solutions to their plight. If the Third World does not go communist, it will go Trotskyist, Nasserist, Socialist, Fidelista, or "Tupamaro"; but it will not retain the status quo which our military-industrial complex espouses.

Our hope for survival, then, rests not on the power that comes from the barrel of a gun but on the powers of humanism and social progress. It is precisely because the military-industrial complex is the greatest enemy of social change that its existence, far from assuring our defense, threatens our survival. To control it or cut it down to smaller dimensions is of some value, but a limited one, because the complex has within it the impulse for resurgence. Control can be useful only if it is a planned precursor to dismantling the complex entirely. If, as this essay has tried to show, the militarist alliance is *counterproductive* — destructive of democracy and a partial cause of war — it is inconsistent to talk simply of making it smaller. Small or large, it serves the wrong purpose.

To dismantle the military-industrial complex is obviously a mammoth task far broader than action by legislators to whittle the defense budget. It calls for the formation of a popular countervailing power to that of the power elite, and for a political campaign of letters, protests, lobbying, and demonstrations, around which that popular alliance can be molded. As we see it, a campaign to alter American strategy toward a humanistic national goal will pivot around three themes:

1. Relative to the communist world, including China and Cuba, a strategy for competitive coexistence.

2. Relative to the world revolution, a strategy for helping it achieve its potential in terms of social progress and freedom.

3. Relative to our own society, a strategy for completing the American revolution.

Specifically, as a tentative and by no means complete counterprogram to that of militarism, the following transition measures seem to be in order:

1. All military aid to foreign nations should be terminated, on the theory that by and large it only helps dictators entrench themselves. Moreover, our military aid creates in its wake subarms races between weaker powers. If the United States had not armed both India and Pakistan, Israel and Jordan, Honduras and Salvador, the armed clashes in those areas might have been mitigated or made impossible.

2. Economic aid should be increased, and the basis for giving it fully altered. Instead of making it conditional on military alliances, military bases, and a willingness to fight communism,

it should be made conditional on *social change.* To the extent that any country needing help — whether communist or non-communist — were willing to introduce social reforms it would be eligible for such aid. If it were taking steps toward economic and political democracy, such as land reform, tax reform, educational reform, labor reform, and the extension of democratic prerogatives, it would receive American largesse to further its revolution. If it weren't taking such steps it would not. In other words, consonant with the strategy of aiding rather than hindering the revolution of rising expectations, economic aid would be exchanged for native reform instead of military advantage or concessions to U.S. business.

3. As quickly as possible aid to foreign nations, as well as a host of other functions, should be progressively funneled through the United Nations. As now constituted the U.N. is a long way from being the embryo of world government. But it will never become such an embryo unless and until individual nations, and in particular the stronger ones, are willing to yield to it part of their sovereignty. The objection to yielding sovereignty is an understandable one: citizens take pride in their own nation's traditions and history, and are loath to dilute that pride by becoming "world citizens." But in an age where a man-made satellite goes around the planet in 90 minutes and where supersonic bombers on the drawing boards are expected to travel at 1,800 miles an hour, eventual unification into a single state is inevitable. History shows that sovereignty progresses with innovations in transport, into ever larger units. The difficulty of travel under feudalism favored the survival of small fiefdoms and duchies. With the industrial revolution, the steamship and the "iron horse," came the modern nation-state. The next step, though it may take time in coming, is virtually predestined. As the world population soars from three and a half to six or eight billion by the end of the century, and as man begins to scavenge the oceans and space for food, minerals, and perhaps water (de-salinized), the boundaries between nations will become less and less meaningful.

4. The United States government should buy out large Ameri-

can firms overseas — in effect nationalizing them — and replace them with government-to-government ventures. This is clearly a drastic step running against the free enterprise tradition, but it is a necessary one to support the revolution of rising expectations.

It isn't that private U.S. investors pay less wages or offer poorer social benefits; on the contrary, as already noted, they usually pay more and provide better fringes than local businesses. But more and more the Third World countries recognize the negative effects of foreign goliaths on their soil. The foreign corporations are interested primarily — as might be expected — in their profits, and only peripherally in developing the weaker states. They use their power therefore to pressure the native regimes for their own ends. For instance, when Venezuela made it known that it did not intend to renew oil leases due to expire in the 1980s, foreign companies retaliated by reducing their purchase of Venezuelan steel. The foreign firms invariably prefer — and give material support to — conservative regimes which allow them higher profits and place less restrictions on them than native or radical ones. Above all, the foreign firms distort the order of economic priorities and inhibit planning. An American company, for instance, may produce automobiles or television sets to make life more pleasant for the middle classes, when it would be more advantageous to the native regime to use the capital and resources for items needed by the lower classes or needed for the infrastructure — telephones, dams, roads, schools, electrification. As already noted (in chapter 2) Mexico's seizure of the foreign oil firms was a necessary precursor to industrialization, for it permitted Mexico to electrify, build 40,000 kilometers of highways, and gain a greater control over its economy.

The United States can significantly stimulate development in the weaker countries by purchasing the facilities of its larger private investors abroad and turning them into what may be called "50-50 companies." Uncle Sam would supply the initial capital, the administrators, and engineers. It would manage the operation while native personnel were being trained to replace the Americans. It would take out its investment from profits over a period, say, of 10 to 20 years; and finally relinquish its own shares to the native government.

Such a program, though not exactly in this form, was adopted by Britain and Burma in the Burmese mining industry, and by Israel and Ghana for Ghanaian shipping. It is admittedly not a widely-tested plan, but it has obvious advantages over both *private* foreign operation and native nationalization. It provides much-needed capital and know-how that the local regime lacks, and it gives it final control over its national resources.

5. A pivotal part of the humanistic foreign policy should be the encouragement and underwriting of *internationhood*. Scores of small countries will never become economically viable — Jamaica, Panama, Syria, the Cameroons, to name a few. Others would be far better off if they didn't have to duplicate industries — steel or auto assembly for instance — for which they have inadequate markets, or which neighbors next door have already developed. Even the most developed nations, as the common market in Western Europe indicates, can benefit from steps toward internationhood. There is obviously a need in all sections of the world for customs unions between neighboring countries and, subsequently, unification into a single "nation." Technology imposes the need for a Pan-Middle East, a Pan-Africa, a Pan-Central America, a United Southeast Asia, a United South America, etc.

Economic and political integration, however, is a painful process in its initial stages. A clothing industry in Country A, for instance, may be highly efficient and one in Country B inefficient and uncompetitive. A customs union would drive the clothing industry in Country B out of business in short order, and reduce its employees to unemployment. In the transition period, therefore, the strong world powers will have to provide the moneys to cushion the shock — to establish new industries, retrain workers, provide unemployment compensation.

6. If military power no longer serves political purposes it has served for centuries, and in fact is counterproductive, it is obviously essential to move toward disarmament. The very idea raises hackles among statesmen and citizens alike; they feel

"naked" without bombs and tanks. The common rebuttal is: "What if the Russians invade us *after* we disarm?"

But this fear is not as rational as it sounds. To begin with, disarmament, if it comes, will probably be multilateral — by pacts negotiated between all the major nations. This is certainly the most desirable form of disarmament, and if it is effected that way it will relieve anxieties that one nation has so much advantage over the other it can invade it. The anxieties will be further relieved if there are simultaneous steps toward internationhood.

If multilateral disarmament proves difficult, however, it seems evident that *unilateral* disarmament is preferable to continuing the present arms race. The arms race is destined to lead America and the world to a nuclear war — with almost mathematical certainty. Few people, if any, would survive. Disarmament by the United States alone, by contrast, at least offers the *hope* of survival. It would certainly not make us less secure than we are now, with nuclear holocaust staring us in the face continuously. And if the Soviets were so foolish as to invade the United States while it was disarmed, it would suffer the same fate — or worse — that France suffered in Algeria, France and the United States in Vietnam. It is inconceivable that American youth would refuse to fight for national independence — either with Gandhian nonviolence or through guerrilla warfare — as Vietnamese youth have done.

There are, we know, standard rejoinders to this thesis — e.g. "Suppose the Russians just bombed us out of existence?" If the Soviets are so insane as to bomb the United States into oblivion without any political or economic purpose, then clearly there is no hope for the policy of deterrence either — for that, too, as every government spokesman has stated repeatedly depends on both sides remaining sane enough to understand the dangers confronting them. Under any circumstance, the risk in unilateral disarmament is far smaller than the risk in the arms race. If we continue on the present path, there is the danger of war by accident, there is the danger of war initiated by many other powers now capable of manufacturing nuclear devices, there is the danger of war resulting from inflamed national emotion or military pressure for a "first strike" because "now we can win."

The United States, of course, does not have to choose unilateral disarmament. If it opts for multilateral disarmament, it can take a number of steps to reduce tensions and create an atmosphere of trust in which negotiations can be fruitful. Up to now each side has proposed that the other give up something considered by it to be vital, while it give up something considered secondary. For instance, the Soviets demand that Washington give up its foreign bases; Washington demands total inspection. A willingness by either side to give up something *important* would soon induce the other to respond.

The United States could certainly dispense with its CBW weapons and most of its nuclear bombs, and still have enough left over to destroy the Soviet Union and China. The Holifield Committee in June 1959 estimated that a Soviet attack with 1,446 megatons (equivalent to a billion and a half tons of dynamite) would kill 50 million Americans and injure 20 million more; presumably an American attack of similar proportions would achieve near-equal results. At that time the United States was said by leading scientists to have 25 to 30 times that amount of megatonnage; today, 10 years later, it must have far more. Obviously, then, there is considerable leeway for the United States to begin the process of disarmament, while seeking meaningful negotiations.

7. Finally, an alternate policy to militarism would include steps to complete the American revolution at home. The specific measures for abolishing poverty, racism, insecurity, are beyond the scope of this book. It is, however, not only morally right that this revolution be completed, but strategically indispensable. It is clear from our recent past that even in the richest nation on earth there can be no such thing as guns *and* butter. Guns create a power elite that denies butter to the poor and oppressed, that refuses to abolish poverty and racism.

The policy of militarism centralizes power more and more in an autocratic state and denies it to the people — to the point where Presidents arrogate to themselves, as individuals, the right to declare war. The "garrison state" is the final alternative in our times to the "humanistic state."

As of now a considerable majority of the American people would reject this seven-point program as "unrealistic," "visionary," "utopian," and what have you. The sloth of the past always exerts pressure on the present. But if America will look at itself honestly it will discover a nation beset by fear, fear that others "want our money," fear of change, fear of thinking — as Einstein suggested — in a new way.

We live, however, at the crossroads of three great revolutions — technological, military, and social. Our very genius can be our undoing unless we abolish war and oppression; but it can lead us, on the other hand, to new vistas of hope, affluence, and security if we apply that technology to life-oriented projects.

Sanity is the application of intelligence to the need for survival. The first step in that direction, it seems to me, is the dismantling of the military-industrial complex.

Notes

CHAPTER ONE

1. J. W. Fulbright, "The Great Society Is a Sick Society," *The New York Times Magazine*, Aug. 20, 1967.

2. *Reviews of Data on Science Resources*, National Science Foundation, No. 14, April 1968.

3. *New Republic*, Nov. 24, 1962, p. 19.

4. *Reviews of Data on Science Resources, op. cit.*, No. 12, Jan. 1968. Also *Federal Funds for Research, Development, and Other Scientific Activities*, Vol. XVII, National Science Foundation, p. 5.

5. Andrew Hamilton, "High Flying in the Pentagon," *New Republic*, May 31, 1969, p. 16.

6. Quoted by Senator Joseph Clark, "Farewell to Arms," *Trade Union Courier*, Jan. 1967.

7. *Chicago's American*, July 17, 1967.

8. N. D. Houghton, ed., *Struggle Against History* (New York: Simon and Schuster, 1968), p. xxxii.

9. *Congressional Record*, Vol. 115, No. 42, p. S2518.

10. Quoted in the *Congressional Record, ibid.*, p. S2519.

11. For these and most of the other data that follow see Senator Proxmire's speech, March 10, 1969, *Congressional Record, ibid.*, pp. S2518 ff., and Report of the Subcommittee on Economy in Government, "The Economics of Military Procurement," May 1969, *Milwaukee Journal*, June 15, 1969.

12. See Amaury de Riencourt, *The American Empire* (New York: Dial Press, 1968), pp. 292-93.

13. *Congressional Record,* Jan. 31, 1969, p. S1125.

14. *Newsweek,* June 9, 1969, p. 79.

15. *Congressional Record,* May 1, 1969, Vol. 115, No. 71, p. S4461.

16. *Congressional Record,* March 24, 1969, Vol. 115. No. 50, pp. S3072 ff.

17. John M. Swomley, Jr., *The Military Establishment* (Boston: Beacon Press, 1964), p. 107.

18. *Congressional Record,* May 5, 1969.

19. *I. F. Stone's Weekly,* July 28, 1969.

20. Richard F. Kaufman, "As Eisenhower Was Saying," *The New York Times Magazine,* June 22, 1969.

21. *The New York Times,* April 9, 1969.

22. See *The New York Times,* Oct. 10, 17, 1945; and D. F. Fleming, *The Cold War and Its Origins, 1917-1950* (New York: Doubleday, 1961), Vol. I, p. 323.

CHAPTER TWO

1. *NSIA Newsletter,* June 1969.

2. *New York Post,* Feb. 11, 1965.

3. R. W. Van Alystyne, *The Rising American Empire* (New York: Oxford University Press, 1960), p. 1.

4. Francis Wharton, ed., *The Revolutionary Diplomatic Correspondence of the United States, 1889,* Vol. II, p. 667.

5. Richard B. Morris, ed., *Encyclopedia of American History* (New York: Harper, 1953), p. 193.

6. Quoted by Albert K. Weinberg, *Manifest Destiny* (Chicago: Quadrangle, 1963), p. 428.

7. See Robert A. Divine, ed., *American Foreign Policy* (Meridian Books; New York: The World Publishing Company, 1960), pp. 127 ff.

8. See Fred J. Cook, "Juggernaut, the Warfare State," *The Nation,* Oct. 28, 1968, pp. 284-85.

9. *Ibid.,* quoted p. 290.

10. D. F. Fleming, *The Cold War and Its Origins* (New York: Doubleday, 1961), p. 1060.

11. Joseph Alsop, *New York Herald Tribune*, July 12, 1946.

12. Quoted by Fleming, *op. cit.*, Vol. I, p. 182.

13. For more details see Sidney Lens, *The Counterfeit Revolution* (Boston: Beacon Press, 1952), pp. 178 ff.

14. David Horowitz, *The Free World Colossus* (New York: Hill & Wang, 1965), p. 85.

15. William Appleman Williams, *The Tragedy of American Diplomacy* (Cleveland: World Publishing Co., 1959), p. 166.

16. *Ibid.*, pp. 167-68.

17. Fleming, *op. cit.*, p. 436.

18. Percy W. Bidwell, "Raw Materials and National Policy," *Foreign Affairs*, Oct. 1958, pp. 144-45.

19. N. D. Houghton, ed., *Struggle Against History* (New York: Simon and Schuster, 1968).

20. Lewis Broad, *Winston Churchill: A Biography* (New York: Hawthorn), p. 186.

21. Quoted by Peter Wiley, "Vietnam and the Pacific Rim Strategy," *Leviathan*, June 1969, p. 42.

22. Houghton, ed., *op. cit.*, p. 49.

23. *Leviathan*, *op. cit.*, p. 5.

24. *Ibid.*

25. Dr. Herbert J. Schiller, "The Use of American Power in the Post-Colonial World," *Massachusetts Review*, Vol. 9, No. 4.

26. Gabriel Kolko, *The Roots of American Foreign Policy* (Boston: Beacon, 1969), p. 64.

27. *Christian Science Monitor*, Dec. 9, 1966.

28. *Columbia Journal of World Business*, Vol. 1, Fall 1965, p. 23.

29. *Steel Labor*, July 1969, p. 4.

30. Houghton, *op. cit.*, p. 142.

31. "Mexico Today," pamphlet published by First National City Bank, Mexico City.

32. Houghton, *op. cit.*, pp. 141-42.

33. For further details see my article in *National Catholic Reporter*, April 4, 1969.

34. June 13, 1961.

35. Amaury de Riencourt, *The American Empire* (New York: Dial Press, 1960), pp. 96-98.

36. *Trade Union Courier*, Jan. 1967.

CHAPTER THREE

1. Quoted by Arthur A. Ekirch, Jr., *The Civilian and the Military* (New York: Oxford, 1956), pp. 22-23.

2. *Conscription News*, Feb. 2, 1956. Also *Progressive*, Jan. 1959, p. 5.

3. "Press Agents of the Pentagon," National Council Against Conscription, July 1953, p. 48.

4. Fred J. Cook, *The Nation, op. cit.*, p. 286.

5. *Current Issues*, Fellowship of Reconciliation, March 1967.

6. *The New York Times*, May 9, 1951.

7. *Chicago Daily News*, April 15, 1969.

8. *Congressional Quarterly*, May 23, 1969, p. 760.

9. *Minneapolis Tribune*, April 1, 1969.

10. *Ibid.*

11. Quoted by Erwin Knoll, "The Military Establishment Rides High," *Progressive*, Feb. 1969, p. 17.

12. *Chicago Sun-Times*, June 15, 1969.

13. Quoted by John M. Swomley, Jr., *The Military Establishment* (Boston: Beacon, 1964), p. 103.

14. *Congressional Quarterly*, May 24, 1968, p. 1167.

15. Quoted, *ibid.*

16. Quoted in *Congressional Record*, Aug. 20, 1968.

17. *Congressional Record*, May 20, 1969.

18. David M. Shoup, "The New American Militarism," *Atlantic Monthly*, April 1969.

19. *Congressional Record*, April 22, 1969, p. S4007.

20. *Congressional Record*, March 20, 1969.

21. Interview July 22, 1969.

22. *The New York Times*, July 8, 1969.

23. *Congressional Quarterly*, March 21, 1969, p. 410.

24. Discussed, *Minneapolis Tribune*, April 1, 1969.

25. *I. F. Stone's Weekly,* July 28, 1969, p. 3.
26. *The New York Times,* June 27, 1969.
27. Senate Hearings on Appropriations. Department of Defense, 1953, p. 1771.
28. John M. Swomley, Jr., "Our Military Government." National Council Against Conscription, Pamphlet, p. 13.
29. Report of the Congressional Conference on the Military Budget and National Priorities, June 1, 1969, pp. 30 ff.
30. *Chicago Daily News,* Aug. 12, 1969, p. 6.
31. *Washington Post,* Dec. 8, 1968.
32. *St. Louis Post-Dispatch,* March 12, 1969.
33. Berkeley Rice, "The Cold-War College Think Tanks," *The Washington Monthly,* June 1969, pp. 22 ff.
34. Quoted in "The Militarization of America," National Council Against Conscription, Jan. 1968.

CHAPTER FOUR

1. *Chicago Sun-Times,* Dec. 7, 1962.
2. "The Economics of Military Procurement," Report of the Subcommittee on Economy in Government, of the Joint Economic Committee of Congress, May 1969, pp. 22 ff.
3. *Washington Post,* June 18, 1969, p. A2.
4. *Congressional Quarterly,* March 14, 1969, p. 369.
5. Senate Committee on Foreign Relations, Hearing on Defense Department Sponsored Foreign Affairs Research, May 9, 1968, p. 97.
6. *Ibid.,* p. 49.
7. *The New York Times,* April 26, 1966, p. 1.
8. Mankiewicz-Braden column, *Chicago Sun-Times,* Aug. 4, 1969.
9. *Chicago Sun-Times,* July 12, 1969.
10. Mankiewicz-Braden, *op. cit.*
11. *Chicago Sun-Times,* Aug. 9, 1969.
12. Flora Lewis, *ibid.,* July 16, 1969.
13. Hans J. Morgenthau, "Congress and Foreign Policy," *New Republic,* June 14, 1969, p. 18.
14. Report of the Congressional Conference on the Military Budget and National Priorities, June 1, 1969, p. 53.

15. For this whole story, see Christopher Morris, *The Day They Lost the H-Bomb* (New York: Coward-McCann, 1966), pp. 10, 32, 46-47, 89.

16. *Ibid.*, pp. 41-42; Morris gives a list of these accidents in which nuclear bombs have been lost.

17. Quoted in "The Militarization of America," National Council Against Conscription, Jan. 1948, p. 13.

18. David M. Shoup, "The New American Militarism," *Atlantic Monthly*, April 1969.

19. Tad Szulc, *Dominican Diary* (Bell Books; New York: Farrar, Straus & Giroux, Inc., 1966), pp. 64 ff.

20. Tad Szulc and Karl E. Meyer, *The Cuban Invasion* (New York: Ballantine Books, 1962), pp. 66-69.

21. Quoted in *Congressional Record*, Jan. 17, 1966, speech by Congressman Donald Rumsfeld.

22. *Washington Star*, Nov. 17, 1966.

23. "The McCarthy Record," Wisconsin Citizens Committee on McCarthy's Record, p. 85.

24. *Look*, Sept. 7, 1954.

25. *Washington Star*, March 24, 1969.

26. Speech reprinted, *Congressional Record*, Oct. 3, 1968.

27. *The New York Times*, Aug. 4, 1947.

28. Defense Department Sponsored Foreign Affairs Research, Hearing Senate Committee on Foreign Relations, May 9, 1968, p. 1.

29. *Ibid.*, p. 16.

CHAPTER FIVE

1. *The New York Times*, July 30, 1969.

2. David Horowitz, *The Free World Colossus* (New York: Hill and Wang, 1965), p. 418.

3. Marvin E. Gettleman, ed., *Vietnam, History, Documents and Opinions on a Major World Crisis* (Greenwich, Conn.: Fawcett, 1965), p. 295.

4. The March 20, 1966 issue of *Chicago Sun-Times* carries a whole series of similar statements by Lyndon Johnson, p. 6.

5. *Christian Century*, June 25, 1945. Also Amaury de Riencourt, *op. cit.*, pp. 150, 216.

6. Senator Joseph Clark, "Farewell to Arms," *Trade Union Courier*, Jan. 1967, p. 2.

7. *Washington Post*, July 1, 1965.

8. C. Wright Mills, *The Causes of World War III* (New York: Simon and Schuster, 1958), p. 47.

9. David Wise and Thomas B. Ross, *The Invisible Government* (New York: Random House, 1964), p. 33.

10. David M. Shoup, "The New American Militarism," *Atlantic Monthly*, April 1969.

11. Rowland Evans and Robert Novak, *Lyndon B. Johnson, the Exercise of Power* (New York: New American Library, 1966), p. 511.

12. D. F. Fleming, *op. cit.*, pp. 922 ff.

13. For details see my articles in the *Progressive*, Dec. 1966, and the *National Catholic Reporter*, April 9, 1969.

14. Statement of Charles L. Schultze before the Subcommittee on Economy in Government, June 3, 1968.

15. Richard J. Barnet, *Intervention and Revolution* (Cleveland: World Publishing Co., 1968), p. 228.

16. *Ibid.*, pp. 248 ff.

17. Senate Committee on Foreign Relations Hearings on Nonproliferation Treaty, Feb. 18, 20, 1969, p. 509.

18. *Chicago Sun-Times*, June 15, 1969.

19. *Chicago Daily News*, June 4, 1969.

20. *The New York Times*, July 23, 1969.

21. Report to U. N. Secretary U Thant by the Task Force on Nuclear Arms Escalation, reprinted in *Saturday Review*, Dec. 9, 1967.

22. Roscoe Drummond and Gaston Coblentz, *Duel at the Brink* (New York: Doubleday, 1960), p. 121.

23. Chalmers M. Roberts, *The Reporter*, Sept. 14, 1954.

24. Edgar Kemler, *The Nation*, July 17, 1954, pp. 45 ff.

25. *Chicago Sun-Times*, Sept. 19, 1966, p. 18.

26. Theodore C. Sorensen, *Kennedy* (New York: Harper, 1965), p. 757.

27. Arthur Schlesinger, Jr., *A Thousand Days* (Boston: Houghton Mifflin, 1965), p. 852.

28. Robert Kennedy, "Thirteen Days, a Personal Story About How the World Almost Ended," *McCall's*, Nov. 1968, p. 149.

29. Irving Louis Horowitz, "Games, Strategies and Peace," American Friends Service Committee, 1963, p. 12.

30. Morton Kondracke, "Washington's Whispered Issue: Our First Strike Capability," *The Washington Monthly*, June 1969, p. 17.

31. *Ibid.* for this and most of the ensuing quotes on damage-limitation.

32. *Ibid.*, p. 20.

33. Andrew Hamilton, "The Arms Race: Too Much of a Bad Thing," *The New York Times Magazine*, Oct. 6, 1968.

34. Schultze, *op. cit.*

CHAPTER SIX

The material in this chapter is taken in large part from three articles by me in *The Nation, Progressive,* and *New Politics.* See "Lovestone Diplomacy," *The Nation,* July 5, 1965; "Labor and the CIA," *Progressive,* April 1967; "Labor Lieutenants of the Cold War," *New Politics,* Summer 1968.

1. *The New York Times,* Aug. 2, 1969.

2. Letter from Lloyd A. Haskins to Ernest Lee, May 2, 1968.

3. UAW press release May 7, 1967. Also private interview July 1969.

4. Dan Kurzman, *Washington Post,* June 14, 1966.

5. B. J. Widick, "Strong Arm of the Status-Quo," *The Nation,* Dec. 27, 1965.

6. *Washington Post,* April 28, 1969.

7. *Free Trade Union News,* Aug. 1969, p. 4.

8. *Washington Post,* April 28, 1969.

9. *Progressive,* Oct. 1966, p. 9.

CHAPTER SEVEN

1. *Chicago Sun-Times,* March 5, 1969.

2. *Chicago Daily News,* Aug. 12, 1969.

3. Mike Klare, "The Military-Education Complex," Liberation News Service, June 1969.

4. Seymour M. Hersh, *Chemical and Biological Warfare, America's Hidden Arsenal* (Anchor Books; New York: Doubleday, 1969), p. 139.

5. Federal Funds for Research, Development and Other Scientific Activities, Vol. 17, National Science Foundation, pp. 28, 31, 215-17.

6. "The University Arsenal," *Look*, Aug. 26, 1969. Also Federal Support to Universities and Colleges, Fiscal Year 1967, National Science Foundation, pp. 50-51.

7. Quoted by Edward Greer, "The Public Interest University," *Viet-Report*, Jan. 1968, p. 5.

8. *Philadelphia Inquirer*, May 16, 1969.

9. Quoted by Carl Davidson, "The New Radicals in the Multiversity," SDS, May 1968, p. 7.

10. Quoted by Michael Klare, "The University and Secret Research," *Viet-Report*, June-July 1967, p. 38.

11. Hersh, *op. cit.*, pp. 189, 192.

12. *Free Trade Union News*, Aug. 1969, p. 4.

13. Hersh, *op. cit.*, pp. 185-86.

14. *Viet-Report*, June-July 1966, p. 40.

15. Michael Klare, "Universities in Vietnam," *Viet-Report*, Jan. 1968, p. 14.

16. Michael Klare, *ibid.*, p. 37.

17. Robert Scheer, "How the United States Got Involved in Vietnam," Center for the Study of Democratic Institutions, 1965, pp. 34-37. Also Martin Nicolaus, "The Professor, the Policeman and the Peasant," Part II, *Viet-Report*, March-April 1966, pp. 5-7.

18. *Christian Science Monitor*, April 25, 1969.

19. Quoted in *The Guardian*, Sept. 20, 1969, p. 7.

20. James Ridgeway, *The Closed Corporation, America's Universities in Crisis* (New York: Ballantine Books, 1969), p. 135.

21. *Ibid.*

22. Ruth Gemis, "The University Arsenal," *Look*, Aug. 26, 1969, p. 35.

23. Hersh, *op. cit.*, p. 188. Also *The University-Military Complex, a Directory and Related Documents*, North American Congress on Latin America, p. 5.

24. Ridgeway, *op. cit.*, p. 133.

25. Hersh, *op. cit.*, pp. 198-99, footnote.

26. Gemis, *op.cit.*

27. Ridgeway, *op. cit.*, pp. 63 ff.

28. *Science*, May 30, 1969, p. 1039.

29. *The University-Military Complex, op. cit.*, pp. 25-27.

30. Gemis, *op. cit.*

31. *The University-Military Complex, op. cit.*, p. 6. Also Ridgeway, *op. cit.*, pp. 216 ff.

32. *Chicago Daily News*, April 11, 1969.

33. Gemis, *op. cit.*

34. Seymour Hersh, "20,000 Guns Under the Sea," *Ramparts*, Sept. 1969, pp. 41 ff.

CHAPTER EIGHT

1. Quoted by Derek Norcross, "Senator Proxmire Seeks to Reverse National Priorities," *Parade*, Aug. 3, 1969, p. 6.

2. *The New York Times*, Aug. 22, 1969.

3. *Ibid.*, editorial page.

4. *Progressive*, Oct. 1961, pp. 14-15.

5. *Chicago Daily News*, Sept. 19, 1969, p. 19.

6. Derek Norcross, *op. cit.*

7. Report of the Congressional Conference on the Military Budget and National Priorities, June 1, 1969, pp. 8, 11-13.

8. John Kenneth Galbraith, *How to Control the Military* (Signet Books; New York: The American Library, Inc., 1969), p. 82.

9. "The Power of the Pentagon," *Progressive*, June 1969, pp. 15, 17.

10. Quoted by Richard J. Barnet, *Intervention and Revolution* (Cleveland: World Publishing Co., 1968), p. 264.

11. *Chicago Sun-Times*, Aug. 19, 1969.

12. *Ibid.*, Sept. 22, 1969, p. 8.

13. Arnold J. Toynbee, *America and the World Revolution* (New York: Oxford University Press, 1962), p. 92.

14. George F. Kennan, *Russia and the West Under Lenin and Stalin* (Boston: Little, Brown and Co., 1960-61), p. 32.

15. Walter Duranty, *USSR, the Story of Soviet Russia* (Philadelphia: Lippincott, 1944), pp. 57-58.

16. Kennan, *op. cit.*, p. 117.

17. D. F. Fleming, *The Cold War and Its Origins, 1917-1950* (New York: Doubleday, 1961), p. 549.

18. Quoted by Hans J. Morgenthau, *Defense of the National Interest* (New York: Knopf, 1951), p. 257.

19. Foster Hailey, *Half of One World* (New York: Macmillan, 1950), p. 51. For this entire section see my *Futile Crusade, Anti-Communism as American Credo* (Chicago: Quadrangle, 1964).

20. *Anatomy of Anti-Communism*, American Friends Service Committee (New York: Hill and Wang, 1969), p. 110.

21. Herman Kahn, *Thinking About the Unthinkable* (New York: Horizon Press, 1962), p. 59.

22. Quoted by Theodore C. Sorensen, *Kennedy* (New York: Harper, 1965), p. 276.

Index